TRANSAMERICA

TRANSAMERICA

SCREENPLAY AND COMMENTARY BY DUNCAN TUCKER

A Newmarket Shooting Script® Series Book

NEWMARKET PRESS • NEW YORK

FIRST EDITION

10 9 8 7 6 5 4 3 2 1

ISBN-13: 978-1-55704-732-8
ISBN-10: 1-55704-732-4

Library of Congress Catalog-in-Publication Data available upon request.

QUANTITY PURCHASES

Companies, professional groups, clubs, and other organizations may qualify for special terms when ordering quantities
of this title. For information, write to Special Sales, Newmarket Press, 18 East 48th Street, New York, NY 10017;
call (212) 832-3575 or 1-800-669-3903; FAX (212) 832-3629; or e-mail info@newmarketpress.com.
Website: www.newmarketpress.com
Manufactured in the United States of America.

OTHER BOOKS IN THE NEWMARKET SHOOTING SCRIPT® SERIES INCLUDE:

OTHER NEWMARKET PICTORIAL MOVIEBOOKS AND FILM BOOKS INCLUDE:

*Includes Screenplay

CONTENTS

FOREWORD

BY JOE MORGENSTERN

Duncan Tucker's *Transamerica* stars Felicity Huffman as Bree, a trans-sexual woman who came into this life as a boy, and who is soon to undergo surgery that will put an end, or so she hopes, to the anguish of her "gender dysphoria." I don't mean to seem cavalier about Bree's plight, but this debut feature left me in a state of movie euphoria. Who would have guessed that such a discomfiting premise would blossom into a deadpan-hilarious and yet deeply affecting story about a singular glitch in the human condition?

The title, as befits the subject, has a dual meaning: the transit from one gender to another—as tortuous a journey as a soul can take—as well as a transcontinental journey prompted by a call, from an inmate of a New York City jail, that reaches Bree at her modest cottage in a working-class area of Los Angeles. The caller, a young street hustler named Toby, claims to be Bree's son. Her son? Well, not exactly. Rather, his son, the product of a hetero-sexual indiscretion when Bree was still a he named Stanley. At this moment in her life, days away from the fateful surgery, Bree wants no part of her accidental parenthood. But her mind is changed by a plot turn that seems per-fectly logical in the surreal circumstances—a therapist's insistence on her confronting her past before the operation that will finally seal it.

Subsequent events are, in their daft way, just as logical. Suffice it to say that Bree flies east, posts bail and drives back west with her scruffy son, who doesn't have a clue, at least at the outset, to the identity of the prim, pedan-tic woman behind the wheel. The scenery is great, thanks in part to Stephen Kazmierski's cinematography and to the endlessly changing countryside; it's not by accident that the United States has produced the world's best road-trip films. But the essence of the adventure is the transformation, against all odds and oddities, that these two lost souls work on one another.

JOE MORGENSTERN is the film critic of the *Wall Street Journal,* in which this review was published December 2, 2005.

Toby, a marvelously sleazy pansexual creep played by Kevin Zegers, goes from bad to worse to better than one could imagine under the influence of Bree's caring, and respect. (Or, from wanting to give up hustling because it's "degradable" to hanging his hat on a twisted branch of the movie industry.) He isn't interested in questions of sexual identity, or, for that matter, in identity, which for him is an iffy thing. Still, Toby, who sometimes looks like a butch Joan Fontaine, keeps poking at Bree until she comes to terms with the persona that she's patched together for herself. And what a persona it is—elaborately false, weirdly stiff, the fragile emanation of an other-worldly creature who dresses conservatively for success, though her vestigial masculinity almost betrays her, and who speaks English with an elegant diction that might have been learned in another galaxy, though it's actually the result of 10 years of college without a degree.

And what a magnificent performance it is. Felicity Huffman, who plays the relatively grounded Lynette on *Desperate Housewives*, makes it clear from the start that Bree is connected to reality by a gossamer thread. ("Goodnight, pretty," she purrs to the ambiguous self in her bedroom mirror.) Yet the actress finds ample room within Bree's desperation for stirring displays of courage, self-irony and romantic longing. If all of these qualities seem too disparate to fit together, that's because the daring filmmaker, Mr. Tucker, chose to write his character that way. This heroine is a work in erratic progress. The oft-heard rationale of those who seek to change their gender through surgery is that they feel they were born into the wrong bodies. Once you've seen Ms. Huffman's Bree you'll believe it.

ON MAKING TRANSAMERICA

BY DUNCAN TUCKER

Shepherding *Transamerica* from concept to script to pre-production to shooting to post-production was like shouldering a boulder uphill. After we finished post I was still shouldering the boulder—at festivals, at events, for press, for promotion. It took a year to write, three years to find the money, a year to go from pre-production through post, and another year to take it from festivals through distribution. I've never worked harder in my life. It's been a wild and amazing ride. But it's also been stressful, scary, and utterly discombobulating. I've never been more surrounded by people, and at many times I've never felt lonelier. My inner compass has been sorely tested. It's not a journey I would recommend to anyone who's not completely committed to the story they're trying to bring to life. (In other words—to make a movie, you pretty much have to be committable.)

When I first set out to write and direct *Transamerica,* I had little idea what I was getting myself into. I never went to film school, which I sometimes say is my strongest suit as a filmmaker. But I love stories and pictures and music. I kept telling myself if I scrunched them all together, somehow a movie would come out.

My brother Robert made a feature film a couple of years ago called *Final Rinse.* He got it done, made the movie he wanted to make and found joy in the process—and he was an inspiration to me. Once I decided I was going to make *Transamerica*—and I mean really make it, come hell or high water—I made a deal with myself: no second-guessing the decision, and no overwhelming myself with too much worrying about everything that lay in store. (I had made a short film, *The Mountain King,* in 2001, but that was a matter of a crew of about four people and a mini DV camera.) When in the beginning I tried to imagine the whole enterprise—all the details, the time, the money, the overwhelming burden of it all—I would feel a rising surge of panic. So I allowed myself to close my mind to the big picture. Thinking ahead one or two steps at a time was enough.

Whenever things got particularly hairy, I brought my mind and heart back to my story and my characters. I thought of them as my children and that kept me going. You'd do anything for your kids, right?

I'm often asked where I got the idea for the movie. There was no "Eureka!" moment. I thought hard about what stories I love the most. And I came up with *Huckleberry Finn*, *The Wizard of Oz*, and *Lord of the Rings*. Then I asked myself, "What do these stories have in common?" The answer: they're all adventure-quest stories, about a hero who goes on a journey to achieve a goal, encounters friends and enemies, and comes back home changed. So I had a template. I was going to make *Lord of the Rings* on a budget. All I had to do was lose the magic and turn Middle-Earth into cross-country America.

I was also thinking and feeling through some important issues in my life, and I knew I wanted to explore those in my screenplay. At the time I began to think about *Transamerica,* I had just lost my father. He was an accomplished man with many friends, yet as he lay dying, it was clear that the most important thing in his life was his family: his wife and three sons. Though I was the oldest son, I always felt like the outsider in my family—a role that may have been more self-imposed than forced upon me. I've always been drawn to outsider characters: the misunderstood, the rejected, the misfits of the world. Fine, I thought. A cross-country America *Lord of the Rings* about a misfit coming to terms with family. I was beginning to imagine a quintessential outsider, someone like James Dean, as Frodo.

The final element clicked into place when a woman I know sat me down one evening and told me that what was under her skirt wasn't what I thought was under her skirt. I'd had no idea—at first I actually thought she was kidding. Then she lowered her voice for me from a pleasant contralto to a deep bass—and reality shifted. Coming out to me was an act of trust and of courage. She shared stories about her life that were sometimes harrowingly sad, sometimes hilarious, and sometimes both at the same time. I was moved and enthralled by our conversation that night. Over the next several months I read extensively and I talked at great length with a number of trans women, and the character of Bree began to evolve.

I worked on the screenplay for about nine months. I did a couple of readings, both of them with wonderful actors. (Laila Robbins and Keith Nobbs at Nuyorican Fifth Night series, and Barbara Sukova and Billy Kay in a private reading, at which I met Linda Moran and Rene Bastian of Belladonna, who would join my old friend Sebastian Dungan in producing.) Finding financing was the inevitable next step. Sebastian and Linda and Rene knocked on every door—all the usual and a few unusual suspects—trying to find backing for the movie. And for nearly three years those doors were politely but firmly closed in our faces. People didn't understand the screenplay. Was it a comedy or a drama? (Yes!) Why did I want a woman to play a trans woman, since obviously trans women are actually guys, and look like guys in dresses? Or my favorite: "Nice script. Call us when you get Meryl Streep."

At some point it became clear that *Transamerica* would never get made unless family and friends helped out. So I talked to my mother, my brothers John and Rob, and several good friends. I scraped together as much as I could from as many sources as I could talk into foolishly backing me, and as part of my come-hell-or-high-water plan, I decided I didn't have the mental energy to worry about the years of work I'd be in for to repay them if the whole thing turned out to be a flop.

My producers Linda, Rene, and Sebastian were brilliant: they actually figured out a way for us to get the movie made for the funds (best described as "extremely limited") I'd managed to collect. I'm indebted to all my collaborators, and count myself lucky to have worked with a cast and crew with such an abundance of craft, creativity, and passion.

I wanted to offer the role of Bree to an actress whom I'd first seen in David Mamet's play *Cryptogram*, produced off Broadway in New York some years before: Felicity Huffman. Felicity is an actress of great intelligence and presence. She's funny, resourceful, sharp-witted, and tender-hearted. She disappears into the skin of the characters she plays. With the help of casting director Eve Battaglia, we sent the screenplay and an offer to her. Felicity responded to the script, and within a few weeks she and I were discussing the project on the phone. We had a great talk and got along well, and by the end of that first phone call she said she was in.

Almost the next thing Felicity told me was that she had a TV show to shoot in fourteen weeks. That was not good news to me. I didn't know if we could possibly get through pre-production and production in that limited time. We hadn't figured out schedules, locations, hired crew, or cast other actors. And I wanted at least six weeks to shoot. I got on the phone with my producers, and after some quick calculations they said we could finish principal photography in time for her TV commitment if we started pre-production immediately. As in that very day. That very hour. I made a bee-line for the production office.

The next eight weeks were something of a blur. I knew some of the actors I wanted for supporting roles: Fionnula Flanagan, Elizabeth Pena, Graham Greene. Eve got busy making offers and auditioning actors for other roles. We limited our location scouting to two parts of the country I was familiar with: upstate New York and Arizona. I had some rough ideas of roads and towns and lakes and landscapes that would work for the movie, and that saved us a lot of time. (As well as money—the Phoenix house belongs to my mom, the Dallas trans house belongs to my friend Lynn Laurino, Calvin's ranch came to us through my friends Patti and Ben Kimball.) I interviewed and hired department heads, the department heads assembled their crews, the director of photography and I designed a shooting plan…the list goes on and on. Linda and Sebastian and Rene were flawlessly dedicated and professional. I would wake up and they would tell me what I was doing that day, and I would do it for about sixteen hours, then go to sleep (if I was lucky), and the next day it would start all over again.

Transamerica managed to attract talent we couldn't afford. People I wanted to work with agreed to sign on to the project at a fraction of their normal rates. Steve Kazmierski, who shot one of my favorite movies, *You Can Count on Me*, was one of the first to come aboard. I knew I wanted to shoot *Transamerica* on super 16 with a very steadily hand-held camera. I wanted the immediacy and intimacy of hand-held, but without excessive jiggle. And I wanted a classical filmmaking language. The camerawork was to be as invisible and natural feeling as possible, so nothing would distance us from Bree and Toby. I liked the way this old-fashioned yet new-fangled camera approach resonated with the old-fashioned yet new-fangled story and central character. Steve understood what I was talking about immediately, and his creative contribution throughout filming was invaluable.

When I met Danny Glicker, our brilliant costume designer, he didn't talk to me about styles or looks or fabrics. He talked about Bree's self-protectiveness, her determination and fragility, her heroism. He talked about Toby as a lost boy looking for a home, and about his imaginative life of Indians and wizards and magic. Danny is deeply talented, and I hope to work with him again and again. (In February 2006, Danny won the Costume Designers Guild Award for Excellence in Contemporary Film for *Transamerica*.)

Mark White, our production designer, made miracles happen on a budget of fifty cents. Lynn Campbell, our key make-up artist, came to us directly from *Sex in the City* to help create Bree's extraordinary face. Jason Hayes, our brilliant wig builder and hair designer, made us two human hair wigs at a fraction of their cost. (He stripped much of the hair out of the wigs so that Bree would look like someone who started transition later in life, after Stanley's hair had started to thin.) Michelle Baker worked wonders finding and managing locations for us. Gaffer Jason Velez, key grip Bob Izzo, sound guru Griffin Richardson—these guys are all heroes, and I am deeply indebted to them.

Jumping ahead to post-production, Pam Wise, who edited *Secretary* and won the Eddy Award for the documentary *Dancemaker*, signed on as our picture editor. Pam is an editor of superb instincts, imagination, and humor. She's inspired in her grasp of character, timing, rhythm, music, and even the importance of the odd but perfectly placed sound effect that somehow makes a difficult moment come alive. *Transamerica* wouldn't have been *Transamerica* without her.

Music Supervisor Doug Bernheim worked miracles to assemble and clear the rights to the great array of country and roots music that's on the soundtrack. Special thanks to Duncan Sheik, Larry Sparks, Jeff Hanna and all the Nitty Gritty Dirt Band, Lucinda Williams, Old Crow Medicine Show, Miriam Makeba, and of course Dolly Parton.

Our composer, David Mansfield, not only wrote the score, but performed it. He played fiddle, guitar, mandolin, dobro, percussion, and about half a dozen other instruments. He's an accomplished studio musician and has played with about every singer and band you can think of, starting with Bob Dylan's Rolling Thunder Revue when David was only a kid. I wanted to ground Bree and Toby in a traditional American sound, in music that would both reflect their journey and identify them as a couple of Americans searching for home in a long tradition of American wanderers. David got it right away. See the scene notes section for more on David and his music.

The work of my actors speaks for itself. I will always be grateful to

Fionnula, Elizabeth, Graham, and Burt for their talent and heart and humor. I hired Kevin Zegers after an extensive search. He was actually one of the earlier actors I saw, but I was prejudiced against casting him because he was so damned pretty. But his audition was great, and he was sweet and sensitive and intelligent and vulnerable, and he understood Toby's damage and his dreams. In the end I managed to find it in my heart to forgive Kevin's perfection. And Kevin found it in his heart to bring to vivid life a lost boy who hasn't yet given up hope. William H. Macy, Felicity's husband, became a friend and adviser during shooting and, when he saw a rough cut of the movie, consented to sign on as executive producer. He was a great help and a great asset to the film.

We started shooting *Transamerica* in late May 2004. We were able to shoot in roughly chronological order, beginning with the scenes in New York City. When you direct a film you've got to be captain of the ship, to set the tone, to convey confidence and excitement and passion—even when you're full of doubt and uncertainty. I had jumbo-sized butterflies in my stomach every day of that shoot. More than anything, I fought for more shooting time with the actors—it killed me when we lost light and had to wrap a scene before I was ready. On our tight six-week schedule, we didn't have much luxury for multiple takes, but I was dogged about giving my actors as much room as possible and about doing everything in my power to help them find their very best work.

★ ★ ★

Transamerica draws its life and soul from the people whose story it tells. I chose to make it a road movie because I wanted to show my two extraordinary main characters against a backdrop of ordinary America and Americans. Bree and Toby unwittingly pioneer new territory in their own lives as they travel from the Northeast to the Southwest, and the sweep and scope of the landscape they pass through mirror their interior journeys. It's impossible to tell a story like this without honoring the tension implicit in the characters and situation. But Bree and Toby remain spirited, hopeful people. I tried to make their story swift-paced and funny, with a lively sense of adventure and of possibility.

Transamerica is a movie about self-acceptance, love, and connection. It's a family values movie. Bill Macy calls it a sheep in wolf's clothing. When we first tried to sell the finished product, several sales agents and distributors, unaccustomed to main characters like Bree, asked us in bewilderment who the movie was for. This always amazed me; it amazes me still.

I believe *Transamerica* is a movie for anyone who's ever felt different and alone. For anyone who's discovered growing up is hard to do. For anyone who yearns to connect. For anyone with a crazy family. For anyone who likes to laugh. For anyone who understands that though it may bring as much pain as it does joy, tearing down the barricades that fear, betrayal, and disappointment erect around our hearts is the only way to live.

TRANSAMERICA

by
Duncan Tucker

Shooting Script
5/15/04

DEEP STEALTH "FIND YOUR FEMALE VOICE" VIDEO

    Excerpts from a vocal training video. ANDREA JAMES, a
    transsexual woman, gives lessons on finding a female voice.

INT. BREE'S APARTMENT - DAY

    BREE OSBORNE (40ish), a prim and proper transsexual woman,
    studies her tonsils in a hand mirror as she practices her
    voice exercises. Her apartment's decorated on a tight budget
    in floral patterns of watermelon and mint. A fertility
    goddess, anthropology texts and women's wear catalogues vie
    for space on the coffee table.

INT. BREE'S BEDROOM - DAY

    MONTAGE: An African war chant plays on the soundtrack as Bree
    dons her battle armor: foundation garments, bra inserts, a
    catalogue-ordered pastel pink outfit, make-up. We don't see
    her face until the end, when she applies a final touch of
    lipstick. She smiles tentatively at her reflection.

EXT. BREE'S APARTMENT - DAY

    Bree walks briskly out. A broad sun hat and sunglasses
    conceal her face. Her femininity is a little over-rehearsed,
    yet she carries herself with a nervous, fragile dignity.

    She lives in a Hispanic neighborhood. Kids play in the
    street, housewives chat on the sidewalk. Bree doesn't meet
    anyone's eyes.

                    DR. SPIKOWSKY (V.O.)
              Any suicidal tendencies?

                    BREE (V.O.)
              No.

                    DR. SPIKOWSKY (V.O.)
              Have you ever felt as though you
              were being followed?

                    BREE (V.O.)
              No.

                    DR. SPIKOWSKY (V.O.)
              Any history of family mental
              illness?

                    BREE (V.O.)
              No.

>   DR. SPIKOWSKY (V.O.)
>   Medical procedures to date?

>   BREE (V.O.)
>   The usual electrolysis, three years
>   of hormone therapy, and facial
>   feminization surgery. Brow lift,
>   forehead reduction, jaw
>   recontouring and a tracheal shave.

5   EXT. BUS STOP - DAY   5

Bree arrives at a crowded bus stop bench. A HISPANIC MAN nods
at her. Bree realizes she's taller than he is. She bends her
knees and slumps.

>   DR. SPIKOWSKY (V.O.)
>   You look very authentic.

>   BREE (V.O.)
>   I try to keep a low profile, blend
>   in. I believe the slang terminology
>   is "living stealth".

6   INT. PSYCHIATRIST'S OFFICE - DAY   6

BREE sits stiffly across from DR. SPIKOWSKY, a weary
psychiatrist working a long shift in an outpatient clinic.

>   DR. SPIKOWSKY
>   Do you consider yourself a happy
>   person?

>   BREE
>   Yes.

Dr. Spikowsky starts to write a note.

>   BREE (CONT'D)
>   No.

Dr. Spikowsky pauses, then again starts to write.

>   BREE (CONT'D)
>   I mean, I will be.

>   DR. SPIKOWSKY
>   Miss Osborne, there's no such thing
>   as a "right" answer in this office.

                    BREE
          Yes. I'm a very happy person.

                    DR. SPIKOWSKY
          How can I help you if you won't be
          honest with me?

                    BREE
          You can sign that consent form.
          Please.

                    DR. SPIKOWSKY
          The American Psychiatric
          Association categorizes gender
          dysphoria as a very serious mental
          disorder.

                    BREE
          After my operation not even a
          gynecologist will be able to detect
          anything out of the ordinary about
          my body. I will be a woman. Don't
          you find it odd that plastic
          surgery can cure a mental disorder?

Dr. Spikowsky writes another note.

                    DR. SPIKOWSKY
          How do you feel about your penis?

                    BREE
               (giving up)
          It disgusts me. I don't even like
          looking at it.

                    DR. SPIKOWSKY
          What about friends?

                    BREE
          They don't like it either.

                    DR. SPIKOWSKY
          I mean, do you have the support of
          friends?

                    BREE
          I'm very close to my therapist.

                    DR. SPIKOWSKY
          And your family?

                    BREE
          My family is dead.

Bree smiles tautly as Dr. Spikowsky makes another note.

7   INT. BREE'S BATHROOM - NIGHT   7

Bree takes two pills from a bottle, swallows them.

                    BREE
              (singing to "You Take the
              High Road")
          You take some hormones and I'll
          take some hormones and I'll be a
          woman before you-

She's wearing a modest lacy nightgown. She notices a slight
but definite masculine bulge in the mirror.

                    BREE (CONT'D)
          Shit. I mean darn.

She practices the more feminine expletive as she carefully
tucks the bulge into a lower-profile position.

                    BREE (CONT'D)
          Darn, darn, darn, darn.

She checks her profile again. Much better.

                    BREE (CONT'D)
          Good night, Bree. Sleep tight,
          Bree.

She straightens a crooked photo of African women who have
beautified themselves with ranks of metal chokers on their
artificially stretched necks.

8   INT. MEXICAN RESTAURANT - DAY   8

A curvaceous WAITRESS walks through a dining room crowded
with Hispanic customers. She enters the kitchen. FERNANDO,
the cook, wolf-whistles at her. Bree stands alone in a nook
off to one side, washing dishes.

Rolling her eyes, THE WAITRESS picks up her order and sashays
out. Bree sways her hips in imitation as she plunges dishes
into scalding water, burning her hands.

9   INT. BREE'S APARTMENT - DAY   9

Bree, prim and proper in another pastel outfit, sits on her
flowered sofa. She consults a printout, dials the phone.

                              BREE
                    Hello, may I speak to Mr. or Mrs.
                    Bhumibol Niratpattanasai? Mrs.
                    Niratpattanasai, this is Bree
                    Osborne with a special offer from
                    the National Home Shopping Club...
                    Hello?... Hello?

She hangs up. The phone rings.

                              BREE (CONT'D)
                    Hello?...I'm sorry, Stanley Schupak
                    doesn't live here anymore. Who's
                    calling?...Stanley doesn't have a
                    son. You must have the wrong...How
                    old are you?...Why don't you call
                    your mother?

Her face frozen, Bree hangs up the phone. She hesitates,
pulling herself together. She consults her clipboard, picks
up the phone and dials.

                              BREE (CONT'D)
                    Hello, may I speak to Mr. or Mrs.
                    Jomal Niang? Mr. Niang, this is
                    Bree Osborne calling with a special
                    offer from the National Home
                    Shopping... Hello?

10   EXT. SHOT - SMALL UPSCALE PROFESSIONAL SUITES BUILDING   10

        Establishing shot.

11   INT. MARGARET'S OFFICE - DAY   11

        Bree walks in. Like a child with a straight "A" report card,
        she holds up the psychiatric consent form for MARGARET, her
        compassionate and thoroughly womanly therapist.

                              BREE
                    He signed it.

                              MARGARET
                    Congratulations.

        Margaret signs the form as Bree anxiously watches.

                              MARGARET (CONT'D)
                    I hereby pronounce you officially
                    legal for sexual reassignment
                    surgery.

                    BREE
Thank you. I- I just- Thank you.

                    MARGARET
So - what else is new?

                    BREE
I made my sales quota for the month
on Tuesday. That pink lamb's wool
cardigan I ordered arrived. Oh, and
this is odd. I got a phone call
last night from a juvenile inmate
of the New York prison system. He
claimed to be Stanley's son.

                    MARGARET
No third person.

                    BREE
My son.

                    MARGARET
I thought you told me you were a
virgin.

                    BREE
I am. There was this one girl at
college but the whole thing was so
tragically lesbian that I didn't
think it counted.

                    MARGARET
Wow. A son.

                    BREE
An alleged son. He's probably just
some sort of scam artist.

                    MARGARET
What is he scamming you for?

                    BREE
Well I guess we'll never know.
Nothing, I mean nothing is going to
stop me from checking into that
hospital next week. I'm not going
to get dragged back into Stanley's
old life.

                    MARGARET
Stanley's life is your life. Why
don't you get in touch with the
mother?

                    BREE
          She's dead. Anyway he's practically
          eighteen - old enough to take care
          of himself.

                    MARGARET
          Bree - this is a part of your body
          that cannot be discarded.

A beat. Bree doesn't know what to say to this.

                    MARGARET (CONT'D)
          I don't want you to go through this
          metamorphosis only to find out
          you're still incomplete.

                    BREE
          What if I visit him later, after my
          surgery. After I've settled into my
          new life.

                    MARGARET
          When you're ready.

Margaret picks up the psychiatric consent form.

                    BREE
          What are you doing?

                    MARGARET
          I can't give this to your surgeon
          right now.

                    BREE
          Yes you can! Margaret, I can't miss
          my surgery on Friday, they're
          booked up a year in advance. I'll
          wire bail money to New York.
               (off her silence)
          I'll call a social worker and have
          someone check in on him. What do
          you want me to do?

                    MARGARET
          All I want is for you to be ready.

Bree gapes at Margaret, reeling with shock.

12   EXT. PROFESSIONAL SUITES - DAY   12

Bree storms out of Margaret's office.

13   INT. BREE'S APARTMENT - NIGHT   13

Bree listens to her stereo: a soprano sings a mournful aria. Bree slows the turntable with one finger. The voice gets deeper, more and more like a man's. Bree makes a decision; there's no way she's going to go back to being a boy. She goes to the phone and dials information.

> BREE
> May I please have the number of the
> New York City adult lock-up?

14   EXT. THE NEW YORK CITY DOWNTOWN LOCKUP - DAY   14

Trying to be as invisible as possible, Bree walks up the steps and into the grey prison building.

15   INT. SERGEANT'S OFFICE - DAY   15

CLOSE UP: Bree Osborne's driver's license up next to a computer display showing the driver's license of a slender man with a moustache. His name is "Stanley Schupak". A SERGEANT looks from one to the other, and then up at Bree.

> SERGEANT
> Can I ask what your relationship is
> to the prisoner?

> BREE
> Allegedly I'm his-
> (she can't bring herself
> to say "father")
> Allegedly, he's my son.

> SERGEANT
> This is his third arrest. They
> always took him to juvenile before.
> This is a new one. According to
> this, he shoplifted a frog.

> BREE
> I beg your pardon?

> SERGEANT
> Plus we have testimony that he was
> in possession of a small amount of
> a suspicious-looking white powder.
> Although emergency services was
> unable to recover the evidence.

                          BREE
            Drugs. I suppose he's an addict?

                          SERGEANT
            Most of them are.

                          BREE
            Most of whom are?

                          SERGEANT
            Mr. Schupak-

                          BREE
            Miss Schupak. I mean Miss Osborne.
            I changed it.

                          SERGEANT
            Do you know that your son's been
            hustling on the streets? Working as
            a prostitute?

                          BREE
            Oh, no. That does it. Absolutely
            not. How much is the bail?

                          SERGEANT
            Bail's set at one dollar.

                          BREE
            I can't possibly afford- One
            dollar?

16   INT. SERGEANT'S OFFICE - DAY   16

        Standing beside a wall of "Wanted" posters, Bree studies her
        face in a compact. A COP comes in escorting TOBY (17), an
        unkempt boy with shadows under his eyes. Toby eyes Bree: a
        conservatively-dressed, middle-aged, erect-spined, schoolmarm-
        mannered woman.

                          COP
            Toby Wilkins, meet Sabrina Claire
            Osborne.

        Bree stares at Toby in dismay. He's surly, dirty and
        dangerous looking. Her worst nightmare.

                          BREE
            My friends call me Bree.

                          TOBY
            Jesus the Reformer?

Bree has no idea what he's talking about.

                    COP
          One of the churches that sends
          missionaries to guide street people
          back to God.

                    BREE
          Oh. No. I'm--

Bree hesitates. She doesn't want to believe she's in any way
connected to this human equivalent of a bad odor.

                    BREE (CONT'D)
          I'm from the Church of the
          Potential Father.

17   INT. NYC COFFEE SHOP - DAY   17

Bree and Toby sit uncomfortably across from one another in a
corner booth. A WAITRESS brings their food. Toby folds his
hands in prayer and waits expectantly.

                    BREE
          Oh - yes... God bless this food,
          and bless this restaurant, and all
          the people in it, and everyone else
          everywhere. Sic transit gloria
          mundi, in excelsis deo. Amen.

                    TOBY
          Do you have any percs? Vicodin,
          anything with codeine?

                    BREE
          Sorry, I'm all out. So why don't
          you tell me something about
          yourself?

                    TOBY
          I'm not naming any names.

                    BREE
          I said about yourself. Is Toby
          short for something? A diminutive?

                    TOBY
          No, it's American.

                    BREE
          Where do you come from?

                    TOBY
Callicoon.

                    BREE
Where's Callicoon?

                    TOBY
In Kentucky. Duh.

                    BREE
Is that where your family is?

                    TOBY
My mother's dead. She had a stroke.

                    BREE
Isn't there anyone else?

                    TOBY
I had a stepfather.

                    BREE
That's wonderful.

                    TOBY
Me and him don't get along.

                    BREE
Why not?

                    TOBY
T.M.I. Too much information.

                    BREE
What about grandparents? Uncles?
Aunts?

                    TOBY
I don't need any family. I can take
care of myself. I'm a loner.

                    BREE
Good for you. That's the spirit.

18   INT. NYC COFFEE SHOP - DAY   18

Later. Bree takes her billfold out of her purse. Toby eyes
her money with interest.

                    TOBY
I've been meaning to thank you for
bailing me out.

                    BREE
          You're welcome.

19   INT. TRANSIENT HOTEL ROOM - NIGHT   19

     Toby unlocks the door, switches on a bare light bulb. Bree
     stands in the doorway, looks over the squalid little room.

                    TOBY
          I decided in jail, I'm giving up
          hustling. It's, like, degradable.

                    BREE
          Degrading. How many people inhabit
          this place?

                    TOBY
          Three. Dude, by the way, I was just
          holding those drugs for a friend.
          I'm not stupid, I've seen what
          drugs can do. Junkies just live for
          the day, no ambition or anything.

                    BREE
          You have an ambition?

                    TOBY
          Yeah. I'm going to get a career in
          the movies.

     Bree sighs, reaches for her purse. She counts out some bills.

                    BREE
          Ten, twenty, forty.

     Toby looks at her pitifully.

                    BREE (CONT'D)
          Sixty, eighty, one hundred. Here.
          Will that hold you for a while?

                    TOBY
          Yeah. Dude, this is great.

                    BREE
          I wish you'd stop calling me
          "dude." Well, I'd best be on my
          way. I've got a flight to Los
          Angeles first thing in the morning.

> TOBY
> Maybe I'll see you out there.
> That's where they make the movies.
> I'm going to hitchhike out there,
> probably, like, tomorrow.

> BREE
> You can't! You don't want to add
> jumping bail to your permanent
> record.

> TOBY
> I'll change my street name.
> Something like Stanley. Stan. Stan
> the Man. That's my dad's name.
> There's his picture. He's with my
> mom.

He shows her a snapshot. Bree leans down to take a look. It's a shot of an awkward looking young couple at a party. The male half of the couple has the same face we saw on Stanley Schupak's driver's license. Bree's knees go weak. She staggers to a chair, sits.

> TOBY (CONT'D)
> Are you okay?

> BREE
> A little dizzy.

She stares at Toby. It's finally penetrating - he's her son.

> TOBY
> Beverly Hills is close to the
> ocean, right? Maybe I'll learn how
> to surf, dye my hair blond for the
> movies. They love blonds. "Blond in
> Blond," "Stocks and Blonds,"
> "Bodacious Blond Bottoms." Not that
> I'm, like, a bottom.

> BREE
> You're talking about pornographic
> films?

> TOBY
> Duh.

> BREE
> Is there a ladies room in this
> establishment?

20   INT. HALLWAY - NIGHT   20

     Bree opens the bathroom door. It's beyond filthy. With a gasp
     she backs away into the hallway.

21   INT. MARGARET'S OFFICE - DAY   21

     The phone rings. Margaret answers.

                         MARGARET
               Hello.

22   INTERCUT: INT. TRANSIENT HOTEL LOBBY - NIGHT   22

     Bree's on a pay phone.

                         BREE
               Margaret? It's Bree. I'm in New
               York. It turns out this whole jail
               episode was just a big mistake.

                         MARGARET
               Talk to me.

                         BREE
               He's a thoroughly independent young
               man. We're getting along famously.
               He's going to come visit me after
               my surgery. I promised I'd take him
               to Disneyland.

                         MARGARET
               I see.

                         BREE
               So I thought I'd catch an early
               flight back tomorrow, get back to
               work, recoup some of the money I've
               lost on this trip before my surgery
               next week. How are you?

                         MARGARET
               Right now I'm a little disappointed
               because you're lying to me. Is
               there anything else you'd like to
               say?

                         BREE
                    (beat; surrendering)
               There appears to be a step-father.
                    (MORE)

                    BREE (CONT'D)
          Perhaps I can effect a reunion.
          Have you ever heard of a place
          called Callicoon?

23   INT. TRANSIENT HOTEL ROOM - NIGHT   23

       Toby opens a large AKC DOG BOOK, slides Bree's hundred
       dollars into a secret pocket he's made by gluing together two
       pages. Bree comes in. He quickly hides the book.

                    BREE
          I just conferred with my immediate
          superior in the church. It seems
          she feels that getting you away
          from this unwholesome environment
          is my moral duty.

24   EXT. NEW YORK CITY STREET - DAY   24

       Toby and ALEX (19), a street hustler, hastily clean out
       Alex's beat-up old junker of a station wagon.

                    TOBY
          Free ride, free food, free motel
          rooms, all the way to L.A.

                    ALEX
          Nothing's free. You'll end up
          marrying her and spending the rest
          of your life eating out cobwebby
          old stank Christian pussy.

       He flashes Toby a glimpse of several glassine bags of heroin.

                    ALEX (CONT'D)
          Something for the road, my man? The
          finest Tecate.

                    TOBY
          Fuck no, man, I'm giving that shit
          up.

                    ALEX
          Only five dollars a bag over street
          price. Convenience charge. We can
          take it out of your cut if she buys
          the car.

                    TOBY
          Fuck you, dude.

                    ALEX
          All right, whatever. You're the
          man.

Toby sees Bree approaching. She stumbles, catches herself,
carries on. Suddenly he's not sure he can face a cross
country trip with her without a little moral support.

                    TOBY
               (turning back to Alex)
          No, wait.

25   EXT. NEW YORK CITY STREET - DAY   25

Bree approaches Alex's grubby station wagon. She looks at it
with distaste. Toby and Alex climb out. She looks at them
with distaste too.

                    TOBY
          I'm not marrying you.

                    BREE
          Glory hallelujah.

Alex pops the hood, shows Bree the filthy motor.

                    ALEX
          Almost new fan belt. I changed the
          oil a couple of months ago, only
          two hundred and thirty thousand
          miles. Just needs a little paint,
          that's all. Runs perfect.
          Guaranteed.

                    BREE
          I've already arranged a rental.

                    ALEX
          But with this one, when you get to
          California you could resell. Make a
          profit.

                    BREE
               (beat)
          A profit?

26   INT/EXT. STATION WAGON - DAY   26

Bree and Toby drive through the industrial sprawl of New
Jersey. Neither looks very happy.

                    BREE
          Fasten your seat belt.

                    TOBY
          I don't like wearing them.

                    BREE
          Well I don't like the idea of
          seeing your internal organs
          splattered all over the dashboard
          if we get into a wreck, God forbid,
          so put it on.

                    TOBY
               (fastening his seat belt)
          See this jacket? It only cost me
          two dollars.

                    BREE
          Quel surprise.

                    TOBY
          And these shoes. Three dollars, a
          dollar fifty each. You know how
          much these things are worth in
          Japan?

                    BREE
          Three dollars?

                    TOBY
          Like 500 dollars. Japanese people
          kill for old Nikes.

                    BREE
          Then you probably should avoid
          wearing them in Japan.

                    TOBY
          Yeah. I'd probably be, like,
          disemboweled by a ninja.

                    BREE
          You don't have to say "like".
          "Probably disemboweled by a ninja"
          is sufficient. And please don't put
          your feet up on the dashboard.

27   INT/EXT STATION WAGON - DAY   27

They drive along a suburban parkway. Toby takes out a
cigarette.

                         BREE
               No smoking in the car.

Irked, Toby puts the cigarette away.

                         BREE (CONT'D)
               I thought instead of driving west
               on 95 we'd wind through the
               mountains on Route 20. Route 20
               takes us close to Callicoon.

                         TOBY
               I don't want to go there.

He turns the radio on. Loud music fills the air. Bree turns
it off. Toby looks daggers at Bree. It's going to be a long
trip.

28   EXT. GAS STATION - DAY   28

Toby watches as Bree pumps gas and washes the windshield.

                         BREE
               What I find absolutely beyond
               comprehension is how a person can
               perform all those intimate acts
               with just any stranger off the
               street.

                         TOBY
               Why should you give a shit?

                         BREE
               Because it's the Christian thing to
               do. How much money did you make
               per...assignation?

                         TOBY
               Forty or fifty dollars. Are we
               going to be going through Texas?

                         BREE
               It's a pretty hard state to avoid.
               It seems like a lot to put yourself
               through for only fifty dollars.

                         TOBY
               That was just my first time.
               Usually I made, like, fifty or
               sixty.
                    (seeing Bree's unimpressed)
               Once I made, like, two hundred.
                         (MORE)

                    TOBY (CONT'D)
          These two guys had me strip and get
          on my hands and knees while they
          watched TV, so they could put their
          beers on my back.

                    BREE
          That's horrible.

                    TOBY
          They used coasters. After the movie
          they hung me upside-down in this
          kind of harness thing-

                    BREE
          Shh! I don't think I need to hear
          the details.

                    TOBY
          And I had to wear this leather mask
          with all these zippers-

                    BREE
          I said I don't want to hear about
          it!

Toby realizes he might have made her think less of him.

                    TOBY
          Anyway, that was like, two months
          ago. I don't do that kind of stuff
          anymore. Can I have some money for
          food?

                    BREE
          What happened to that hundred
          dollars I gave you yesterday?

                    TOBY
          I had to, like, use it to pay the
          rent.

Bree studies him a moment, then hands him the squeegee: dance
for your supper. He grudgingly takes it and starts to clean
his side of the windshield.

29   INT. MINI-MART - DAY   29

A candy bar in his mouth, Toby slips a few dollars between
the pages of his dog book.

30   EXT. STATION WAGON - DAY   30

Sunset. Bree and Toby drive along a country highway.

31   EXT. VIRGINIA MOTEL - NIGHT   31

They pull into the parking lot of a motel.

32   INT. VIRGINIA MOTEL ROOM - NIGHT   32

Toby, wearing only a skimpy pair of raggedy underpants,
adjusts a toy action figure to stand guard on his head-board.
He hears the toilet flush and flops back on the bed. He poses
seductively.

Bree comes out of the bathroom in a concealing robe, holding
a road map. She sees Toby, looks away in discomfort.

                    BREE
          I'm sorry I can't offer you a
          private room. The church has to
          conserve its resources. I've
          charted us a course on the nice
          little red roads. Callicoon is only
          about 45 minutes out of our way.

                    TOBY
          I don't want to go there. These are
          nice beds.

                    BREE
          Don't you have any pajamas?

                    TOBY
          No.

                    BREE
          Well you should get some.

She gets into her bed, covers her eyes with a sleep mask.

                    BREE (CONT'D)
          Good night.

Toby stares at her, feeling confused and rejected.

33   EXT. VIRGINIA MOTEL - DAY   33

Establishing shot. It's morning.

34   INT. VIRGINIA MOTEL ROOM - DAY   34

Light pours in through the window onto Toby's sleeping body.
Dressed and made-up, Bree claps her hands to wake him up.

                    BREE
          Rise and shine. Up up, up. We've
          got a schedule to keep.
              (off his groggy stare)
          Did I put on too much blush?

                    TOBY
          You're weird.

Bree's face falls. Toby heads for the bathroom. Bree walks to
a mirror, checks her face. She touches her breasts,
reassuring herself of who she is and where she's going.

35   INT/EXT. STATION WAGON - DAY   35

They drive through farm country.

                    TOBY
          The first place I lived, this,
          like, hole in the wall off Avenue
          C, I had, like, four roommates. One
          was a junkie, one was a crackhead,
          one was a junkie, and the other one
          was, like, a junkie.

                    BREE
          Like, like, like.

They pass a church with an inspirational message on its
marquee sign: "Welcome All God's Creatures: Thieves, Liars,
Gossips, Bigots, Adulterers, Deviants, Children."

                    TOBY
          Do you believe everything the bible
          says is true?

                    BREE
          Well, I suppose in a metaphorical
          sense.
              (off his look)
          Metaphor. When one thing represents
          or symbolizes another.

                    TOBY
What I don't get is, if Jesus had
all these powers, why didn't he
just use them to like- To escape?

                    BREE
Because death and rebirth is the
whole point of the story. Which
closely parallels the mystery cults
of Mithras and Osiris. It's also,
metaphorically speaking, about the
human capacity for self-
reinvention, transformation and
change.

                    TOBY
Did you know the Lord of the Rings
was gay?

                    BREE
I beg your pardon?

                    TOBY
There's this big black tower,
right? And it points right up to
this huge burning vagina thing, and
it's like the symbol of ultimate
evil. And then Frodo and Sam have
to go into this cave and deposit
their magic ring into this hot
steaming lava pit, only at the last
minute Frodo can't perform, so
Gollum bites off his finger. Gay.

                    BREE
That's a highly original
deconstruction.

                    TOBY
If I could be a wizard I'd want to
be a shape-changer. I could turn
into whatever I wanted. A fish, a
rock, a cow.

                    BREE
Don't you think you'd be a bull?

                    TOBY
I could be a cow if I wanted.

                    BREE
I think I want to be a wizard too.

                    TOBY
          Wizards are only guys.

                    BREE
          That's the most ridiculous thing I
          ever heard.

36   INT/EXT. STATION WAGON - DAY   36

      Toby's asleep. Bree takes an exit off the highway.

37   INT/EXT. STATION WAGON - DAY   37

      MONTAGE: They drive over a wide brown river, under an old
      railway overpass and into a depressed southern town.

38   INT/EXT. STATION WAGON - DAY   38

      Bree pulls to a stop in front of a decrepit, burnt-out hotel.
      Toby's eyelids flutter open.

                    TOBY
          What the fuck are you looking at?

      He sits up, glances outside. And shoots Bree a look of
      disbelief and betrayal.

                    BREE
          I just didn't think it was right to
          come so close without at least
          passing through.

      Toby grabs his knapsack, jumps out of the car. He stalks down
      the street. Bree rolls down the window, shifts into reverse
      to follow him.

                    BREE (CONT'D)
          Toby, where are you going?

      He changes direction. She stops, shifts into drive. Toby
      crosses the street to get away from her. ARLETTY HUBBELL
      (50s), a lively black woman, spots Toby from a doorway.

                    BREE (CONT'D)
          Would you come back here!? You're
          acting like a spoiled child!

      Arletty rushes up to Toby, envelops him in a big hug.

                         ARLETTY
              Oh my God! I can't believe my eyes!
              It's my sweet little angel baby!

39   EXT. THE RIVER ROAD - DAY   39

          Arletty and Toby drive together along a riverfront road. Bree
          follows in the station wagon.

40   INT. ARLETTY'S HOUSE - DAY   40

          Toby and Arletty sit side-by-side on a couch in Arletty's
          living room. The room is full of knick-knacks, photos of
          family and old fishing memorabilia - a shrine to Arletty's
          memories. Bree sits apart in an easy chair.

                         ARLETTY
              Look at you. Give me another hug. I
              could wring your neck like a
              chicken. My favorite boy, and all
              this time not even a phone call to
              tell me if you were alive or dead.

                         TOBY
              I wasn't ever your favorite.

                         ARLETTY
              That's what you think.
                   (to Bree)
              I used to look at him out that
              window, playing all day with that
              big dog of his.

                         BREE
              Toby lived near here?

                         ARLETTY
              Just two doors up the road.
                   (to Toby)
              Now tell me what you've been doing
              with yourself. I want to hear
              everything.

          At a loss, Toby darts a nervous glance at Bree.

                         BREE
              He's been in New York, working
              toward developing a career in the
              film industry.

                    TOBY
          I'm going to California.

                    ARLETTY
          California! Well. He always was the
          artistic type. He used to have this
          precious little stuffed monkey he
          carried around with him everywhere.
          Even to school. Are you in the
          movie business too?

                    TOBY
          She's a missionary. From a church.

                    ARLETTY
          Praise the Lord. I'm an
          electrolygist myself. If you want,
          I could get those couple little
          hairs out from under your nose in
          nothing flat.

Bree's hand flies to her face in horror.

41   INT. ARLETTY'S HOUSE - DAY   41

Arletty works on Bree with a BUZZING needle. Toby eats a
sandwich and potato chips.

                    ARLETTY
          My boss lady down at the salon, she
          used to work out in California.
          From what I hear, some of those
          Hollywood beauties used to be as
          hairy as hogs.

The needle BUZZES one more time. Bree twitches.

                    ARLETTY (CONT'D)
          There. That ought to keep them from
          sticking their heads out again.
               (to Toby)
          You ought to go on over and say
          hello to your step-daddy.

                    TOBY
          I don't want to see him.

                    BREE
          Of course you do. The man raised
          you, fed you, clothed you,
          sheltered you from harm. He's your
          father. For all practical purposes.

Toby stands up and walks out of the room.

> ARLETTY
> He always was a sensitive thing.
> Are you driving him all the way to
> California?

> BREE
> I think I need some air. Excuse me.
> And thank you.

She rises and goes outside.

42   EXT. RIVER ROAD - SUNSET   42

The sun sets over the river.

43   INT. BOBBY JENSEN'S HOUSE - NIGHT   43

A knock on the door. It opens to reveal Bree.

> BOBBY JENSEN
> Yeah?

> BREE
> Do you perchance know a Toby
> Wilkins?

> BOBBY JENSEN
> Who's asking?

> BREE
> I am a bearer of glad tidings. Your
> son has come home.

44   INT. ARLETTY'S HOUSE - NIGHT   44

On the radio, a preacher praises Jesus. Toby builds a house
of cards; Arletty crochets. Bree opens the back door.

> BREE
> Arletty, Toby, I brought back a
> surprise.
>   (beckoning to someone outside)
> Come on in.

BOBBY JENSEN (40s) hesitantly steps in. Toby lurches to his
feet. He stares at Bobby Jensen like a cornered rabbit
staring at a fox.

                    ARLETTY
          Look who's here.

                    BREE
          If you can't bring Mohammed to the
          mountain bring the mountain to
          Mohammed.

                    BOBBY JENSEN
          Wow, look how much you've grown.

                    BREE
          Toby, give your father a hug.

                    BOBBY JENSEN
          I was worried sick about you. Why'd
          you run off like that? Don't you
          know I missed you?

                    BREE
          Isn't this sweet?

Toby doesn't move. Bobby Jensen walks over and hugs Toby, who
stiffly suffers the embrace. And then Toby finds his courage.

                    TOBY
          I know what you missed. You missed
          my mouth. You missed my ass.

                    BOBBY JENSEN
          Hush up now. What're these ladies
          going to think?

                    TOBY
          You want to fuck me right here in
          front of them?

                    BOBBY JENSEN
          Shut up!

Bobby Jensen BACKHANDS Toby. Toby falls to the floor.

                    ARLETTY
          Bobby!

                    TOBY
          Was that good for you? Come on,
          Bobby.

He reaches out toward Bobby Jensen's crotch, talking like a
hustler to a john.

                         TOBY (CONT'D)
              You liked it in the car.

                         BOBBY JENSEN
              Shut up!

Bobby Jensen PUNCHES him. Toby crumples to the floor,
gasping.

                         TOBY
              You liked it in the basement. You
              liked it in the garage.

Bobby Jensen KICKS him. Toby tries to curl himself around
Bobby's legs. Bobby KICKS him again. Bree's frozen in shock.
Bobby raises his fist. And Arletty CLOBBERS him on the head
with Bree's make-up bag. Bobby stumbles, BANGS his head on
the wainscoting. He COLLAPSES, out cold. There's a breathless
silence. Toby reaches out to feel Bobby Jensen's heart.

                         ARLETTY
              Toby? Honey-

Toby scrambles to his feet, lurches out the door. Bree and
Arletty stare after him in shock.

45   EXT. BOBBY JENSEN'S HOUSE - NIGHT   45

Bree and Arletty carry Bobby Jensen's unconscious body. They
heave him onto an old lawn chair.

                         ARLETTY
              This man's heavy with sin. I don't
              know you, Bobby Jensen.

Bobby lets out a loud snore.

                         ARLETTY (CONT'D)
              He'll come to in a couple of hours.

She walks off in disgust. Sounds of someone rummaging in the
garage catch Bree's attention.

46   INT. BOBBY'S GARAGE - NIGHT   46

Bree walks in to find Toby searching through a pile of boxes.

                         BREE
              This isn't my fault! You never told
              me why you didn't want to come
              home!

Toby finds a sleeping bag and a lantern. He angrily stalks past her.

                    BREE (CONT'D)
          Where are you going?

He doesn't answer - just walks outside and disappears into the night. Bree stares after him. She spots an old stuffed toy monkey in a cardboard box - Toby's old toy. She picks it up.

47   EXT. RIVER ROAD - DAY   47

Arletty carries a tray of food into the woods. Toby lies curled up on the ground in the sleeping bag. She kneels beside him.

                    ARLETTY
          Toby? Honey, I brought you some
          breakfast.

48   INT. ARLETTY'S HOUSE - DAY   48

Bree sits staring out the window. She's dressed and made-up. Arletty comes in.

                    ARLETTY
          He's walking down to the highway
          ramp to hitchhike himself a ride.
               (off Bree's silence)
          He's a disappearing act all right.
          This is just what he did after his
          mama killed herself.

                    BREE
          She what?

                    ARLETTY
          She shut herself up in the garage
          with the car on. Toby found her
          there when he got home from school.

                    BREE
          Oh, God.

Bree feels the burden of responsibility settling ever-heavier on her shoulders.

49   EXT. RIVER ROAD - DAY   49

        Toby walks along the road, carrying his knapsack. Bree
        catches up with him in the station wagon. He ignores her. She
        drives alongside him. After a long moment he stops. Bree
        brakes. Toby gets into the car.

50   INT/EXT. STATION WAGON - DAY   50

        They drive through hilly pastureland. Toby sits beside her,
        twigs in his hair.

                        BREE
                Lovely scenery in this part of the
                country.

                        TOBY
                I said I'd take a ride from you. I
                didn't say I'd carry on a fucking
                conversation.

                        BREE
                I was just trying to do you a
                favor. God knows, considering the
                way you've been living your life it
                wasn't unreasonable to try to put
                you under some sort of parental
                supervision.

        Toby reaches into his knapsack, digs out a bag of heroin. He
        scoops out a bump of powder.

                        BREE (CONT'D)
                What's that? Is that drugs? Oh, no.
                Absolutely not.

        Bree brakes suddenly.

                        TOBY
                God damn it!

        He starts over again. Bree reaches for the drugs.

                        BREE
                No! That is not all right! You
                cannot do that here! No!

        There's a moment of struggle. Toby raises a fist
        threateningly.

                    TOBY
        Are you going to let me do my
        thing, or do I have to get out of
        this fucking car right now? Huh??

Bree shrinks from his fist. She's not accustomed to violence.

                    BREE
        Go ahead. Kill yourself. What does
        it matter to me?

51   INT. TENNESSEE ROADSIDE RESTAURANT - DAY   51

Bree and Toby sit at a booth. Toby's lost in a heroin daze. A
WAITRESS brings them beverages.

                    WAITRESS
        One chocolate milk shake, and
        coffee for your mother.

                    TOBY
        She's not my mother.

                    BREE
        I'm not his mother.

The Waitress moves on to another table. Toby burps loudly.
Disgusted, Bree gets up, moves to the next booth.

52   INT/EXT. STATION WAGON - DAY   52

They drive along a road that winds through a valley.

                    BREE
        You have a lot of anger inside you.
        I understand that. Right now you
        probably think drugs are the only
        friend you've got.

                    TOBY
        Are you trying to ruin my get-high?

                    BREE
        I'm just saying maybe we ought to
        start all over, from scratch.
        Hello, my name's Bree. What's
        yours?

Toby turns to stare out the window.

53   EXT. TENNESSEE GAS STATION - DAY   53

Establishing shot.

54   EXT. TENNESSEE GAS STATION - DAY   54

Bree self-consciously pumps gas as some country GREYBEARDS
look on. Toby smokes a joint behind the station. He stubs it
out, pockets it, strolls back to the car.

                    BREE
          I didn't get a wink of sleep. Let's
          find a motel.

                    TOBY
          I'm camping out.

Bree sighs in vexation.

55   INT. TRADING POST STORE - DAY   55

Toby drifts through the fluorescent aisles of a general
store. He comes to a shelf of whiskey, stops, looks around.
He slips a flask into his pants.

Bree's in the camping department, her shopping cart laden
with supplies. A SALES LADY shows her an olive green sleeping
bag.

                    BREE
          Do you have anything a trifle
          less...butch?

56   EXT. TENNESSEE LAKESIDE CAMPSITE - EVENING   56

Bree sets up a camping stove. Toby crouches at the shoreline,
poking the lake bottom with a long stick. Bree takes two
freeze-dried camping meals out of a shopping bag.

                    BREE
          Fettucine Alfredo or chicken cordon
          bleu?

                    TOBY
          Chicken.

                    BREE
          Matches?

Toby takes out his matchbook. It's empty.

> TOBY
> Fuck!

He flings the matchbook away. Bree looks at the stove, her cheap sleeping bag, the desolate surroundings. Her shoulders slump.

> BREE
> Excuse me. I've got to go to the
> ladies room.

She picks up a roll of toilet paper, stands and walks unhappily toward the woods. A beat. She comes back to the campsite.

> BREE (CONT'D)
> Do you think there are snakes
> around here?

Toby looks up, interested at this possibility.

57 EXT. LAKESIDE CAMPSITE WOODS - EVENING   57

Bree BEATS the underbrush with a big stick.

> BREE
> Get away, snakes! Get away, snakes!

58 EXT. LAKESIDE CAMPSITE - NIGHT   58

Toby sits near the glow of his battery lantern. Bree comes up to join him. She sits delicately on her make-up case. Toby takes a swig of whiskey. He hiccups.

> BREE
> Where did you get that?

> TOBY
> I had it.

A loon calls.

> BREE
> What is that awful sound?

> TOBY
> Loon.

                    BREE
          Certain Native American tribes of
          the northern plains believed loons
          were ancestral spirits trying to
          communicate with the physical
          world.

Another loon calls. Both of them shiver.

                    TOBY
          My real dad's part Indian.

                    BREE
          Is he?

                    TOBY
          Yeah. I mean he never told me but I
          just know. It's an Indian thing.

Bree gets out her hormone pills.

                    BREE
          Do you think you could find it in
          your heart to offer a sip of that
          to a lady?

                    TOBY
          Are you sick or something?

                    BREE
          No. These are vitamins.

She takes her pills. Toby hiccups again.

                    BREE (CONT'D)
          When I was a little girl I had a
          terry cloth bunny. I used to sleep
          with her every night.
                    (off Toby's hiccup)
          Try holding your breath. Then one
          day my parents decided I was too
          old for her. I never saw her again.

Bree takes his stuffed monkey from her purse.

                    BREE (CONT'D)
          I found this in your step-father's
          garage.

                    TOBY
          Ohhh...

Toby unsteadily puts down his bottle, takes the monkey. Bree smiles, thinking he's touched. And then he leans into the bushes and VOMITS. Bree recoils in disgust.

> BREE
> Oh, no. Ugh. Here.

She hands him a tissue. He retches sickeningly. Bree awkwardly pats his back. A few repulsive moments later, he finishes vomiting. Wasted, he leans back against her.

> BREE (CONT'D)
> Ugh.

The haunting call of another loon fills the air. Bree can't suppress a shiver. Toby warbles an imitation of the loon's call. He looks weakly up at Bree.

> TOBY
> They're talking to us. We've got to
> talk back.

He tries another imitation. He tugs on her sleeve to get her to join in. Bree gives a half-hearted loon call. LONG SHOT: Toby leans against Bree at the lakeside. Their voices mingle eerily. Toby moans and pukes again.

59   EXT. TENNESSEE LAKESIDE CAMPSITE - DAY   59

60   EXT. LAKESIDE CAMPSITE - DAY   60

Dressed and made-up, Bree shakes Toby's shoulder.

> BREE
> Rise and shine. Come on, let's go.
> I've got to be in L.A. by the end
> of the week.
>   (as he stirs)
> What would you say if I told you I
> could set you up with a job in the
> telemarketing field?

61   INT/EXT. STATION WAGON - DAY   61

They drive through woods and farmland.

                    BREE
          The nice thing about telemarketing
          is, you can live practically
          anywhere. I could drop you off in
          Austin.

                    TOBY
          I'm going to California. My real
          dad has a mansion there. With a
          pool.

                    BREE
          What do you see your life like, ten
          years from now?

                    TOBY
          Probably get a job in a pet store.
          Have a dog. And kids.

                    BREE
          Kids.

                    TOBY
          I always wanted to have kids.

                    BREE
          Perhaps you ought to aim for
          something a little higher than
          working in a pet store. If you like
          animals you could be a
          veterinarian. Or a zoologist.

Toby looks at her, unsure whether she's making fun of him. He
toys with a small charm hanging from a cord around his neck.

                    TOBY
          I'm out of cigarettes.

                    BREE
          Quel dommage. What's that you wear
          around your neck?

                    TOBY
          It's a dog tooth. What's quel
          dommage mean?

                    BREE
          It means you're not getting any
          cigarettes. A dog tooth?

                    TOBY
          It's from this dog I used to have,
          Cookie. To remember her by.
                    (MORE)

                    TOBY (CONT'D)
          She was a good dog. She slept in my
          bed. Bobby shot her.

                    BREE
          He shot your dog?

                    TOBY
          He said she barked too much. She
          did bark a lot, but she was just
          trying to watch out for us.

                    BREE
          He shot your dog.

62   INT. ARKANSAS ROADSTOP CAFE GIFT SHOP - DAY   62

      Toby browses through cheap souvenirs in the gift shop. He
      spots a rack of baseball caps on sale for $3.00 each. He
      finds one with a picture of an Indian. He looks up to see
      TAYLOR (15), a roadstop Lolita, unabashedly checking him out.

63   INT. ARKANSAS ROADSTOP CAFE - DAY   63

      Bree studies the menu. A little girl stares at her intently.
      Ill-at-ease, Bree smiles at her, looks away. Feeling the
      little girl's eyes still on her, she looks up again.

                    LITTLE GIRL
          Are you a girl or a boy?

      Bree settles lower in her chair, wanting to disappear.

64   INT. ARKANSAS ROADSTOP CAFE - DAY   64

      Distraught, Bree dials a number on a pay phone. In the
      background, Toby and Taylor play a video game.

                    BREE
          Margaret? Thank God. I'm in the
          middle of Arkansas and an eight-
          year-old child just read me! I
          can't handle this. I had to camp
          out last night. On the ground. With
          bugs!

      Toby loses the video game. He mutters a curse. Taylor grabs
      his neck and locks lips with him, pulling him close.

                    BREE (CONT'D)
          ...Because he is impossible. I
          can't fritter away my savings like
          this, my surgery's only five days
          away... Dallas? I don't know, four
          or five hours. Why?

She spots Toby and Taylor in heated embrace.

                    BREE (CONT'D)
          Hold on.
               (to Toby)
          Toby? Toby! Would you mind
          introducing me to your new friend?

                    TAYLOR
               (off Toby's hesitation)
          Taylor.

                    TOBY
          Yeah, this is Taylor.

                    BREE
          It's nice to meet you, Taylor.

TAYLOR'S FATHER rounds the corner.

                    TAYLOR'S FATHER
          What's going on here? Come on. Your
          mother's waiting in the car.
               (to Bree)
          You better watch out he doesn't get
          some poor innocent girl into
          trouble.

                    BREE
          You'd better watch out she doesn't
          end up ruining some poor innocent
          boy's life!
               (to Toby)
          You - wait for me at the table.
               (back on the phone)
          Margaret? I really don't think I'm
          cut out to be a mother.

65   INT. ARKANSAS ROADSTOP CAFE - DAY   65

Bree slides into a chair opposite Toby. She opens her mouth
to say something pungent. Toby lowers his head, clasps his
hands expectantly. Bree rolls her eyes, folds her hands with
a sigh.

                    BREE
          Dear God, bless this meal, and
          please help Toby to find the
          strength not to take any more
          drugs, so that when we get to L.A.
          he can get a job and find a nice
          apartment, so even if he never
          finds his real father, he can lead
          an independent life. Amen.

                    TOBY
          Amen. They've got a cool hat back
          there. It's only, like, ten bucks.
          I think my nose is getting
          sunburned.

                    BREE
          Eat your vegetables.

Toby uses his fingers to take a tiny bite of broccoli.

                    BREE (CONT'D)
          You might want to use a fork. Just
          an idea.

Toby picks up his fork.

                    BREE (CONT'D)
          I'll tell you what. You can have
          that hat on one condition. No more
          drugs. I mean it. Deal?

                    TOBY
          Deal.

He reaches across the table to shake her hand.

66   INT. ARKANSAS ROADSTOP CAFE BATHROOM - DAY   66

Toby, wearing his new hat, snorts a bump of heroin.

67   EXT. ARKANSAS ROADSTOP CAFE PARKING LOT - DAY   67

Bree cleans out the mess on Toby's side of the car. Toby
walks up behind her, holding something behind his back.

                    TOBY
          I got you a present.

Bree turns. Toby gives her a baseball cap.

                          BREE
                Thank you. I'm very--

She looks more closely at the hat. In bold letters it
proclaims, "I'M PROUD TO BE A CHRISTIAN".

                          BREE (CONT'D)
                    (dismayed)
                --touched.

                          TOBY
                Put it on.

Bree looks around. She uncomfortably puts on the cap.

                          TOBY (CONT'D)
                It looks good.

68   INT/EXT. STATION WAGON - DAY   68

They drive along an Arkansas highway. Toby leans his body out
the passenger side window at a 45 degree angle, sitting on
the edge of the door. Bree tugs at his shirt.

                          BREE
                Would you get back in here?! Do you
                know how dangerous that is?!

Toby comes back inside, grinning.

                          TOBY
                I was holding on.

                          BREE
                Are you trying to give me a heart
                attack?

                          TOBY
                Did I scare you?

                          BREE
                I suppose that just makes your day.

                          TOBY
                It helps.

Bree frowns at him in exasperation.

69   INT/EXT. STATION WAGON - DAY   69

            MONTAGE: They drive through hills, then flat fields, then
            into the Dallas city limits, then into a pleasant suburban
            neighborhood.

                              TOBY (V.O.)
                    Why are we going to Dallas?

                              BREE (V.O.)
                    An associate of mine has arranged a
                    place for us to stay the night.

70   EXT. DALLAS HOUSE - EVENING   70

            Bree and Toby walk up to the front porch of a handsome house.

                              BREE
                    This Mary Ellen woman is being very
                    generous to offer us her
                    hospitality, so I hope you'll be on
                    your best behavior.

                              TOBY
                    I'm always on my best behavior.

            Bree rings the bell. MARY ELLEN, a tall Texan belle with a
            wide smile, opens the door.

                              MARY ELLEN
                    Sabrina and Toby, right? I'm Mary
                    Ellen. Come on in.

            She looks over their shoulders, shouts to an adolescent
            skateboarding on the street.

                              MARY ELLEN (CONT'D)
                    Justin Duvall, you put on that
                    safety helmet before I tell your
                    mother!

71   INT. DALLAS HOUSE - NIGHT   71

            Mary Ellen leads Bree and Toby in.

                              MARY ELLEN
                    I'm having a little get-together
                    but you two just come on in and
                    make yourselves at home.

In the living room, a small party is in full swing. KELLY, a
pretty young woman, holds up a polaroid.

                    KELLY
          Mary Ellen, come here! Debbie's
          showing us pictures of her new
          vagina!

                    MARY ELLEN
          I'm sorry - they're feeling a
          little bit feisty. Everybody, this
          is Sabrina, and her handsome escort
          here is Toby.

Bree takes a closer look at the guests. Every one of them is
a transsexual.

                    BREE
               (whispering to Mary Ellen)
          Margaret said you were stealth!

                    MARY ELLEN
          I am, in public. But this is the
          privacy of my own home. Welcome to
          the first meeting of the Gender
          Pride President's Day Weekend
          Caribbean Cruise Planning
          Committee.

                    BREE
               (edging backward)
          We've got to go.

                    TOBY
          How do you guys know each other?

                    BREE
          We don't! She's a friend of a
          friend. Of a friend.

                    MARY ELLEN
          There's rum punch in the kitchen,
          and guacamole in the dining room.

                    TOBY
               (to Bree)
          Don't be so uptight. It's a party.

As Bree stands frozen in anxiety, he walks past her to join
the festivities.

72   INT. DALLAS HOUSE - PARTY SCENES MONTAGE - NIGHT   72

--Mary Ellen dances while CALPERNIA plays a jig on the fiddle
and the other guests laugh and clap.

--Mary Ellen brings a cup of punch to Bree, who's still
standing as close to the door as politeness allows.

                    MARY ELLEN
            Margaret said you were planning to
            have your surgery soon.

                    BREE
            Toby doesn't know about me.

                    MARY ELLEN
            You're stealth to him? Don't worry,
            honey - we've all been there. I'll
            pass the word.

73   INT. DALLAS HOUSE (PARTY SCENES MONTAGE) - NIGHT   73

--CALLIE and KELLY subject Toby to an examination.

                    KELLY
            Blunt fingers. Calluses.

                    CALLIE
            High bone mineral density.

                    KELLY
            It doesn't look good.

                    CALLIE
            Strong odor. Gamy.

                    KELLY
            Hair could start falling out any
            day now.

                    CALLIE
            Poor thing. He's got all the
            symptoms.

                    KELLY
            Of what?

                    CALLIE
            Testosterone poisoning.

The women start to giggle.

--Bree listens to a pair of trans lovers: SANDI and MELISSA.

                    SANDI
          It was one of those instant best
          friend things.

                    MELISSA
          But at the time we were both
          straight men. What could you do
          with that?

                    SANDI
          We had our surgery the same day.

                    MELISSA
          We ended up holding hands in the
          recovery room.

                    SANDI
          And now this gorgeous creature is
          the love of my life.

Toby walks up. There's an uncomfortable moment.

                    SANDI (CONT'D)
          We were just telling your friend a
          little bit about the transsexual
          lifestyle.

                    TOBY
               (to Bree)
          Not what you're used to in church,
          is it?

--Sandi, Kelli and FELICIA show two vaginal dilators to Toby.

                    SANDI
          These are vaginal dilators. She
          just had her surgery last month.

                    FELICIA
          This is Keanu Two. And this is
          Keanu Three.

                    KELLY
          Where's Keanu One?

                    SANDY
          Keanu One is in Hollywood filming a
          major science fiction epic, and we
          don't want to hear a snarky remark
          about him.

--DAVID, a mystical female-to-male transsexual, deals tarot cards for Toby.

> DAVID
> We're not gender-challenged. We're gender-gifted. I've been woman and I've been man, and I know things you single sexed people can't even begin to imagine.

> TOBY
> Dude, I thought you were a real guy.

> DAVID
> We walk among you.

--Bree stands with Mary Ellen. Her eyes light on a woman with the face of a lumberjack.

> BREE
> That poor thing couldn't pass on a dark night at two hundred yards.

> MARY ELLEN
> You'd better check your T-dar, honey. She's a G.G.

> BREE
> A what?

> MARY ELLEN
> A genetic girl. From Mary Kay. If you let her do a color trial she'll give you a free compact.

--The guests sit and listen as Mary Ellen sings "Home on the Range", accompanied by Calpernia on the fiddle.

> MARY ELLEN (CONT'D)
> *Oh give me a home, where the buffalo roam, and the deer and the antelope play...*

> CALPERNIA
> *With each other...*

Bree, still holding herself apart from the others, rolls her eyes and walks out of the room.

74   INT. DALLAS HOUSE GUEST BEDROOM - NIGHT   74

We hear party sounds from downstairs. Toby comes into Bree's
bedroom. He spots a bottle of nail polish remover in her make-
up case. He opens it, sniffs deeply and smiles as the fumes
make his head spin.

His eyes fall on Bree's satin nightgown. He picks it up,
holds it up to his shoulders, checks his reflection in the
mirror.

Bree comes out of the bathroom wearing only her bra and
girdle. She spots Toby, squawks in shock, covers her crotch,
spins and ducks back into the bathroom. Toby drops the
nightgown and stumbles against the dresser.

                    TOBY
          Sorry.

                    BREE
          Could you please hand me my robe?
          The pink satin? It's by the...

Toby hands it to her then retreats to the bed. In a moment
Bree comes into the room, belting her robe around her waist.

                    BREE (CONT'D)
          An unfortunate side-effect of my
          pills. They're a diuretic.

                    TOBY
          Gross.

                    BREE
          A diuretic. It makes you go number
          one, not number two. Listen, I'm
          sorry about those ersatz women.

                    TOBY
          What?

                    BREE
          Ersatz. It means phony. Something
          pretending to be something it's
          not.

                    TOBY
          I thought they were nice.
          Zoologists are the guys that work
          in zoos, right?

                    BREE
          Yes. Among other places.

                    TOBY
          I never met my real dad. My mom
          would never talk about him much.
          I'm going to live with him, though.
          When I save up enough money I'm
          going to buy a nice pair of clothes
          and then I'll just knock on his
          door and surprise him. Do your mom
          and dad live in California too?

                    BREE
          My parents are dead.

                    TOBY
          Do you like zoos?

                    BREE
          I don't mind the modern ones I
          guess. The animals may not be free,
          but they're safe, protected from
          all the dangers of the wild.

                    TOBY
          Yeah, me too. Good night.

He walks out.

                    BREE
          Good night.

75   INT/EXT. STATION WAGON - DAY   75

They drive through the wide-open Texas flatlands.

                    TOBY
          Did you go to a college?

                    BREE
          Yes.

                    TOBY
          What did you study?

                    BREE
          A lot of things. French, cultural
          anthropology, archeology,
          psychology, art history.

They pass the squashed body of an animal on the roadside.

                    BREE (CONT'D)
Ugh.

          TOBY
Possum. Biology.

          BREE
Eighty million years ago, during
the Cretaceous period, these plains
were the floor of a huge inland
sea.

          TOBY
Are we there yet?

          BREE
Well, if you don't want to learn
anything, then never mind.

          TOBY
All right, I'm listening.

          BREE
It cut the entire continent in two.
Dinosaurs lived on either shore.
Then a huge meteor struck the
earth. Some people say that's why
the dinosaurs went extinct. But why
should the insects, birds and
mammals have survived?

          TOBY
Why?

          BREE
I don't know, but it always sounded
a little bit fishy to me.

Bree chuckles, pleased with her joke. Toby smiles.

          BREE (CONT'D)
Did you know they've found giant
shark remains in the middle of
Kansas?

          TOBY
How big were they?

          BREE
Big enough to swallow you without
even chewing.

Their voices fade as the car travels on, moving along a road that runs dead-straight over dun-colored plains.

76   EXT. STATION WAGON - SUNSET   76

The car heads directly west, into a dramatic sunset streaking the sky. We hear FART NOISES on the soundtrack.

77   INT/EXT. STATION WAGON - SUNSET   77

His lips on his arm, Toby imitates a particularly gross and noisy fart. Bree looks straight ahead. Toby watches her closely.

                    TOBY
          Got you.

                    BREE
          You did not.

He makes another fart noise. Bree's lips quirk.

                    TOBY
          I got you.

Bree play-hits Toby.

                    TOBY (CONT'D)
          Ouch! You got me in the eye, you
          got me in the eye!

                    BREE
          I'm sorry! Are you all right?

                    TOBY
          I got you.

Bree reaches out and tickles his ribs.

                    TOBY (CONT'D)
          Ow! Stop it! Seriously, watch the
          road.

                    BREE
          You drive. I hope we pass a rest
          stop soon. My diuretic's kicking
          in.

78   INT/EXT. STATION WAGON - NIGHT   78

Toby drives. Beyond the circle of the station wagon's
headlights everything is dark. He pulls to the side of the
road. Bree looks outside nervously. There's six inches of
roadbed, some tall spiky grass and a lot of dark night.

                         BREE
           Do rattlesnakes come out at night?

Toby shrugs. Bree gets out of the car.

79   EXT. STATION WAGON - NIGHT   79

Bree edges to the back of the car. She pulls down her girdle,
raises her dress, squats and pees. What a relief. A coyote
HOWLS. Alarmed, Bree stands - still peeing and fully exposed.
An approaching car rounds the bend.

Inside the car, Toby checks his reflection in the rearview
mirror. The passing car catches Bree in its lights. Toby sees
Bree's reflection - and learns something he didn't know.

80   INT. STATION WAGON - NIGHT   80

Bree gets back in.

                         BREE
           Well, I must say that's a relief.
               (off Toby's silence)
           Toby? Is something wrong?

Toby puts the car into gear and floors the gas.

81   INT. WEST TEXAS MOTEL ROOM - NIGHT   81

Double beds. Bree lies in hers, reading a magazine. Toby's in
his, buried in a comic book. He lights a cigarette.

                         BREE
           This is a no-smoking room.

Toby ignores her. He puffs his cigarette, turns the page of
his comic.

82   INT/EXT. STATION WAGON - DAY   82

Bree drives. Toby stares out the window.

                    BREE
          New Mexico is the ufology capital
          of the world. Ufology, from U.F.O.
          The study of unidentified flying
          objects.
                (off Toby's silence)
          You know, social ostracism doesn't
          work in a community of two.
                (beat)
          Damn it, Toby! Say something!

Toby stares at a hand-painted billboard: SAMMY'S WIGWAM -
REAL INDIAN ARTIFACTS AND SOUVENIRS - 200 YARDS.

                    TOBY
          I want to go to Sammy's Wigwam.

83   INT/EXT. SAMMY'S WIGWAM- DAY   83

A touristy souvenir stand on the roadside. SAMMY sits in a
lounge chair beside tables of cheap Indian headdresses,
Godseyes, peace pipes, sand paintings and other tchotchkes.
Toby checks out a large stone tomahawk.

                    BREE
          Here are some arrowheads. They're
          only a dollar each.

Toby ignores her. Bree turns to Sammy.

                    BREE (CONT'D)
          He's been acting like that all day.

Toby POUNDS the tomahawk violently on the table, then POUNDS
it again, harder.

                    BREE (CONT'D)
          Young man, if you don't start
          behaving in a civilized fashion you
          and I are going to have a very
          serious problem.

                    TOBY
          Fuck you.

                    SAMMY
          Hey - you watch your mouth around
          your mother.

                    TOBY
          She's not my mother. She's not
          anybody's mother.
                (MORE)

                    TOBY (CONT'D)
          She's not even a real woman. She's
          got a dick.
                    (to Bree)
          Don't you? Don't you? Go on, tell
          him!

Mortified, Bree turns and quickly walks with as much dignity
as she can muster the long distance back to the car. Toby
shouts after her.

                    TOBY (CONT'D)
          You're a fucking lying freak!

84   EXT. SAMMY'S WIGWAM - DAY   84

Bree walks to the car. Toby hurries after her.

                    TOBY
          What do you want out of me?

                    BREE
          Just because a person doesn't go
          around blabbing her entire
          biological history to everyone she
          meets doesn't make her a liar.

                    TOBY
          Then why didn't you just tell me
          the truth?

                    BREE
          So you could humiliate me in public
          even sooner?

                    TOBY
          You knew all about me!

Bree gets in the car, slams the door. Toby bangs on her
window. She rolls it down.

                    TOBY (CONT'D)
          Why'd you bail me out of jail?
          What, you just walked into jail,
          asked them who needed help?
                    (off her silence)
          You know what, fuck you. I never
          even heard of a trannie church
          lady. You can drop me off in the
          next town.

He gets in the back seat.

                    BREE
          So you think I don't have the right
          to belong to a church? My body may
          be a work in progress but there is
          nothing wrong with my soul.

She eyes the Christian cap on the dashboard.

                    BREE (CONT'D)
          Jesus made me this way for a
          reason, so I could suffer and be
          reborn, the way he was.

                    TOBY
          So you're cutting your dick off for
          Jesus?

                    BREE
          That's not how it works. I'll just
          have an innie instead of an outie.

                    TOBY
          Eww.

A skinny young dreadlocked HITCHHIKER (20) wearing fatigues
and suspenders, appears at Bree's window.

                    HITCHHIKER
          Hi. Is there any chance you could
          offer a fellow traveler a ride?

Bree shakes her head. Toby opens his door.

                    TOBY
          Sure. We love helping out
          strangers.

85   INT/EXT. STATION WAGON - DAY   85

Bree drives. Toby and the Hitchhiker sit in back.

                    TOBY
          Beef jerky?

                    HITCHHIKER
          No thanks. I'm a level four vegan.
          I don't eat anything that casts a
          shadow.
               (taking out a pot pipe)
          A little token of my appreciation?

                         TOBY
               Absolutely.

The Hitchhiker lights up. Bree rolls down her window. It's
loud and windy at 50 mph.

                         BREE
               I'm sorry, but the secondary smoke
               might render me unfit to drive.

                         HITCHHIKER
               She's cool, right?

                         TOBY
               She's not a she. She's got a dick.

                         BREE
               Toby!!

                         TOBY
               For now at least.

                         HITCHHIKER
               You're a guy?

                         BREE
               I'm a transsexual woman.

                         HITCHHIKER
               Wow. I think transsexuality is a
               radically evolved state of being.

Bree glances at him with sudden interest.

                         TOBY
               Hey, look!

Some ways off the road an arm of an artificial desert lake
sparkles under the hot sun.

86   EXT. ARTIFICIAL DESERT LAKE PARKING SPOT - DAY   86

The station wagon's parked at the lakeside. Bree sits on a
boulder, averting her eyes as the boys strip.

                         BREE
               Many societies throughout history
               have honored and revered
               transgendered people. The Zulu, the
               Yoruba. The Native Americans called
               us two spirit people.

                    HITCHHIKER
          Two spirits. I like that.

                    TOBY
          Tell him what they're going to do
          with your dick.

                    BREE
          Then the settlers came. They tended
          to murder us on sight.

                    HITCHHIKER
          The way the white man treated the
          Indian was very deeply fucked up.

                    TOBY
          Yeah.

                    HITCHHIKER
          Are you sure you won't join us?

                    TOBY
          Come on. We know what you've got.

                    BREE
          You boys go ahead. Have fun.

The boys run whooping toward the water. Bree turns her head
to watch them, a part of her wishing she could be as free.

87   EXT. ARTIFICIAL DESERT LAKE - DAY   87

Bree sits by the shore as the boys swim. The Hitchhiker makes
for a stone outcrop. Toby, less comfortable in the water,
clings to a large piece of driftwood.

                    BREE
          So what do you do when you're not
          following the open road?

                    HITCHHIKER
          I'm a peyote shaman.

                    TOBY
          How do you do that?

The Hitchhiker climbs up the steep outcrop.

                    HITCHHIKER
          Well, it involves consuming
          majestic amounts of peyote.
                    (MORE)

                    HITCHHIKER (CONT'D)
          And then, when you're done throwing
          up, you see things.

The Hitchhiker BACKFLIPS into the water. He surfaces,
gasping.

                    TOBY
          What things?

                    HITCHHIKER
          Once I saw my own death.

                    BREE
          Do you by any chance drown in a
          desert lake?

                    HITCHHIKER
          No. I die in a depressurization
          accident on a moon colony. I'll
          show you something. It's in my bag.

He swims for shore. Bree looks down at Toby.

                    BREE
          Do you still think- What you said
          back at Sammy's Wigwam?

                    TOBY
          What?

                    BREE
          That I'm a freak.

                    TOBY
          You're not a freak.
              (off Bree's pleased smile)
          You're just a liar.

The Hitchhiker runs up to the car, gets in the driver's seat.
Bree and Toby hear the engine start. They look up in shock as
the Hitchhiker drives the car off toward the highway.

                    TOBY (CONT'D)
          Oh SHIT!

                    BREE
          My purse... My hormones! You dirty
          motherfucking hippie!!

                    TOBY
          My dog book was in that car.

88   EXT. NEW MEXICO DIRT ROAD - DAY   88

Bree and Toby walk along the shoulder of the empty road.

                    BREE
          Oh God, oh God oh God. I've got to
          be in L.A. in two days. What are we
          going to do?

Toby pulls out his bag of heroin, shows it to Bree.

                    BREE (CONT'D)
          Is it soothing?

                    TOBY
          I could sell it.

                    BREE
          How much could you get?

A PICKUP approaches. Toby quickly sticks out his thumb. It
slows to a stop.

89   INT/EXT. PICK-UP - DAY   89

Bree and Toby sit in the truckbed with some Mexican laborers.
Bree tries frantically to tie her scarf around her head as
the highway wind plays havoc with her hair.

90   INT. NEW MEXICO DINER - DAY   90

A hangout for locals and truckers. Bree and Toby come in,
looking very out-of-place. Bree hurries toward the bathroom.
Toby follows more slowly, checking out the customers. He
meets and holds the eyes of a middle-aged TRUCKER.

91   INT. NEW MEXICO TRUCK STOP WOMEN'S ROOM - DAY   91

Bree stares in alarm at her reflection. Wind-tossed hair,
dusty clothes, smudged lipstick. With a groan she turns the
tap on full-blast and desperately finger-combs her hair.

92   INT. NEW MEXICO DINER MEN'S ROOM - DAY   92

Toby washes his hands. The TRUCKER enters, steps up to the
sink next to Toby. Toby catches his eye in the mirror and
flashes him an encouraging smile.

93   INT. NEW MEXICO DINER - DAY   93

        Bree comes out of the bathroom, her face scrubbed, her hair
        pulled back. Though she wouldn't believe it, she looks better
        than we've ever seen her. She sits at the counter.

        A half-eaten plate of French fries lies abandoned beside her.
        Beyond the plate she spots tip money. Her eyes on the money,
        Bree reaches out a hand - then meets the gaze of CALVIN
        MANYGOATS (40s), a Native American sitting a couple of stools
        away. Bree takes a French fry.

                        CALVIN
                Having a tough day?

94   INT. TRUCK CAB - DAY   94

        Toby and the Trucker climb into the truck cab. The Trucker
        pushes Toby onto the bed behind the seats.

95   INT. NEW MEXICO DINER - DAY   95

        Bree and Calvin sit side by side.

                        BREE
                I don't care about the car. I just
                need to get to Los Angeles as
                quickly as possible.

                        CALVIN
                Well, I'm driving a couple of good
                ponies over to the sale in Show Low
                in the morning. I could give you a
                ride that far. Hey Woodrow, can I
                get a burger for the young lady
                here?

        Bree blushes like a schoolgirl.

96   INT. TRUCK CAB - DAY   96

        The Trucker pulls Toby's shirt off, reaches for his pants,
        slides them down.

97   INT. NEW MEXICO DINER - DAY   97

        Bree cuts a hamburger neatly in half.

                    BREE
          Calvin. Isn't that an unusual name
          for a Native American?

                    CALVIN
          Not really. My brothers are Dwight,
          Lloyd, Darryl and Woodrow.

                    BREE
          What's your last name?

                    CALVIN
          Manygoats. It's my mother's clan
          name.

                    BREE
          Ah, a matrilineal kinship system.

Calvin doesn't reply. He's not sure what she's talking about.

                    BREE (CONT'D)
          Is there a Mrs. Manygoats?

                    CALVIN
          Not yet. I guess the right woman
          hasn't met me.

Toby walks up to stand beside Bree. His face is flushed and
sweaty.

                    BREE
          There you are. Calvin, I'd like you
          to meet Toby. Toby, this is Calvin
          Manygoats.

                    CALVIN
          Pleased to meet you, son.

                    BREE
          I saved you half a hamburger.
          Calvin's offered us a place to stay
          tonight, and a ride in the morning.
          Isn't that generous of him?

                    TOBY
          I guess.

He looks at Bree meaningfully, jerking his chin toward a
corner of the room. Bree turns to Calvin.

                    BREE
          Excuse us just a minute.

As she rises Calvin stands, a gentleman. Toby leads Bree a few steps away. He proudly shows her a couple of twenties. Bree snatches the bills.

> BREE (CONT'D)
> You already found a buyer? Well at least now you don't have any more of that damn drug.

She reaches to pat Toby on the back. Before she knows it she's giving him an awkward hug. She pushes away from him.

> BREE (CONT'D)
> Shower.

Toby follows her back to Calvin.

> BREE (CONT'D)
> So, Calvin. Have you lived in New Mexico all your life?

> CALVIN
> Not yet.

Bree laughs delightedly. She's never been flirted with before. Toby feels the first pangs of jealousy.

98   EXT. CALVIN'S HOUSE - SUNSET   98

Calvin's old pick-up pulls up to a small house in canyon country. Calvin, Bree and Toby get out.

> BREE
> It's beautiful.

> CALVIN
> It's home.

99   INT. ADOBE BEDROOM - NIGHT   99

Bree lies awake in bed. Toby's in a sleeping bag on the floor. The sounds of someone strumming a guitar float through the window. Bree gets up quietly, tiptoes out. Toby silently watches her go.

100   EXT. ADOBE HOUSE - NIGHT   100

Bree opens the door, waves tentatively at Calvin, who sits on an old lawn chair with his guitar.

                    BREE
          Hi.

Calvin smiles, gestures for her to come outside and join him.
He offers her a big brown bottle.

                    CALVIN
          Mezcal. A friend of mine brings it
          up from Oaxaca every year.

Bree takes a sip, coughs demurely. Calvin starts to sing.

                    CALVIN (CONT'D)
          Beautiful dreamer, wake unto me,
          starlight and dewdrops are waiting
          for thee. Sounds of the rude world
          heard in the day, lull'd by the
          moonlight have all pass'd away...

101   INTERCUT: INT. ADOBE BEDROOM - NIGHT   101

Toby listens to Calvin serenading Bree.

                    CALVIN
          Beautiful dreamer, queen of my
          song, list while I woo thee with
          soft melody. Gone are the cares of
          life's busy throng, beautiful
          dreamer awake unto me, beautiful
          dreamer awake unto me.

                    BREE
          You can sing.

                    CALVIN
          Just enough to keep the dogs off
          the back porch. Here, have some
          more.

He offers her the bottle. Bree takes another sip. She coughs.
And coughs some more.

                    CALVIN (CONT'D)
          That'll put hair on your chest.

                    BREE
          I hope not.

LONG SHOT: Bree and Calvin sit companionably in the dim glow
of the porch light.

102   EXT. ADOBE HOUSE - DAY   102

        Bree watches Calvin load a couple of horses into a trailer.
        Toby comes outside, yawning.

                        BREE
                Good morning, sleepyhead. Guess
                what? Calvin's going to drive us
                all the way to Phoenix.

        Bree examines her breasts.

                        BREE (CONT'D)
                Do my breasts seem smaller to you?
                I've missed two doses of my pills.
                Play with the body's hormonal
                balance and you're playing with
                fire...
                    (practicing her voice)
                Playing with fire. Playing with
                fire.

        She waves at Calvin. He tips his cowboy hat. Bree giggles
        like a schoolgirl. Toby's clearly not happy with this
        situation.

103   INT/EXT. CALVIN'S PICK-UP - DAY   103

        Calvin, Bree and Toby drive down the highway. Calvin
        demonstrates the art of wearing a cowboy hat.

                        CALVIN
                Y'know when you wear your cowboy
                hat if you wear it forward like
                that it means you're looking for
                trouble. If you wear it back like
                that it means you're not looking
                for trouble. And if you wear it off
                to the side it means you're out to
                impress the ladies.

                        TOBY
                How come an Indian wears a cowboy
                hat?

                        CALVIN
                I guess because it keeps the sun
                out of my eyes better than a
                headband and a couple of eagle
                feathers.

                    BREE
          Calvin was telling me his people
          are Navajo.

                    CALVIN
          Part Navajo. My great-great-great-
          grandfather was a Zuni.
                    (to Toby)
          You have a Cherokee look about you.
          Proud people, them Cherokee.

Toby turns to stare out the window. But he can't resist
raising his hand to feel his cheekbone. Cherokee...

104   EXT. DESERT ROADSIDE - DAY   104

Calvin pulls over to the road shoulder to take a break.

105   EXT- DESERT ROADSIDE - DAY   105

Bree, Toby and Calvin sit in the back of the truck, eating
tamales. Calvin fishes a beer out of the cooler. Toby reaches
for one for himself. Calvin kicks the cooler shut.

                    CALVIN
          You're too young.

                    TOBY
          No I'm not.

                    BREE
          Yes you are. Drink some water. Now
          if you gentlemen will excuse me,
          I've got to go to the powder room.

Calvin hands her a roll of toilet paper, helps her down to
the ground. She smiles and heads across the road.

                    TOBY
          Dude, there's things about her
          she's not telling you.

                    CALVIN
          Every woman has the right to a
          little mystery. Dude.

                    TOBY
          Did you know she's a Jesus freak?
          She's probably waiting to convert
          you.

Calvin eyes Bree awkwardly making her way out of sight on the other side of the road, toilet paper held aloft, the breeze catching the tail of the roll and floating it up like a flag.

> CALVIN
> She could convert me anytime she
> wants to.

106   MONTAGE: INT/EXT CALVIN'S PICK-UP - DAY   106

They drive through a ponderosa pine forest, down a series of mountain switchbacks, through Saguaro country on the outskirts of Phoenix.

107   INT/EXT. CALVIN'S PICK-UP - DAY   107

They pull to a stop in front of a mini-mansion in an affluent Phoenix suburb.

> CALVIN
> I wish I could drive you all the
> way to Los Angeles.

> BREE
> So do I.

Toby reaches across Bree, tries to open the door. It's stuck; Calvin gets out and opens it. He offers Bree a hand; she takes it and steps out.

> CALVIN
> Bree, there are things about me you
> don't know, things about my past-

> BREE
> We all have our secrets.

Toby gets out and SLAMS the truck door.

> CALVIN
> I've been in jail more than once.
> I'm about blind in one eye, and
> I've got half a pound of shrapnel
> in my left leg, but--

He hands her a piece of paper with his telephone number.

> CALVIN (CONT'D)
> If you're ever back in New Mexico
> I'd really like it if you gave me a
> call.

                    BREE
          Thank you, Calvin. I'll do that.

They look in each other's eyes a long moment.

                    TOBY
          Come on, let's go.

                    CALVIN
               (to Toby, commandingly)
          Come here.

Toby reluctantly walks back to Calvin. Calvin pulls an old
cowboy hat out of the back of the truck.

                    CALVIN (CONT'D)
          This belonged to a friend of mine.
          He was a champion in the All Indian
          Rodeo circuit.

He pushes the hair out of Toby's eyes, puts the hat on Toby's
head.

                    CALVIN (CONT'D)
          Now you look like a warrior.

With a nod to Bree, Calvin circles around and gets into his
truck. As Bree and Toby watch, he drives off. Bree turns
resignedly toward the mini-mansion.

                    TOBY
          So where are we?

                    BREE
          My parents' house.

                    TOBY
          I thought you said your parents
          were dead.

                    BREE
          Wishful thinking.

108   EXT. PHOENIX HOUSE - DAY   108

Bree guides Toby toward the front door. She hides out of
sight behind a garden wall.

                    TOBY
          Who's Sydney?

                    BREE
          My baby sister. Go on.

Toby rings the bell. He picks his nose. ELIZABETH (60s),
Bree's gorgeous, bird-of-paradise trophy-bride mother, opens
the door.

                    ELIZABETH
          May I help you?

                    TOBY
          Is Sydney here?

                    ELIZABETH
          Sydney's out. May I tell her who
          called?

                    TOBY
          Uhh... I don't think so.

He turns and walks away. Elizabeth shuts the door. Bree
hurries after Toby.

109   EXT. PHOENIX HOUSE - DAY   109

Bree and Toby sit in the scant shade of an ornamental tree.
The heat is oppressive. Toby wipes his brow, sighs, glances
at Bree.

                    BREE
          Don't look at me like that.

                    TOBY
          I'm not looking at you.

                    BREE
          All right, all right. Shit. I mean
          darn. No, I mean shit.

She gathers her scarf and jacket, stands up to face the
inevitable.

110   EXT. PHOENIX HOUSE - DAY   110

Bree rings the doorbell. Bree's father MURRAY (60s) opens the
door.

                    MURRAY
          May I help you young lady?

                    BREE
          Dad, it's me.

Elizabeth appears beside Murray. Her eyes widen. She SLAMS
the door in Bree's face. Bree pounds on the door.

                    BREE (CONT'D)
          Mom! Dad! Mom!

The door reopens and Elizabeth pulls Bree inside.

                    ELIZABETH
          Get in here, before the neighbors
          see you.

She and Murray stare at Bree in astonishment.

                    MURRAY
          Jesus Christ. I can't even
          recognize you.

                    BREE
          It's still me. Only different.

                    ELIZABETH
          So you've done it? It's all over?

                    BREE
          I don't think that's any of your
          business.

Elizabeth reaches out and GRABS Bree's genitals.

                    ELIZABETH
          Thank God, Murray. He's still a
          boy.

Bree stares at her mom. She takes Elizabeth's hand, puts it
defiantly on her breast. Elizabeth jerks her hand away as
though she were touching hot coals.

                    ELIZABETH (CONT'D)
          Oh! My little Stanley. I can't even
          look at you.

Tears welling, she rushes out of the entryway.

                    MURRAY
          Why do you have to always upset her
          like that?

                              BREE
                    I'll tell you what - let me get
                    something to eat and drink, then
                    I'll go back and wait for Sydney
                    outside.

She heads for the kitchen. After a moment, Murray follows
her.

111   INT. PHOENIX KITCHEN - DAY   111

Murray watches Bree make two thick chicken sandwiches.

                              MURRAY
                    Are you sure you're all right,
                    Stanley?

                              BREE
                    Fabulous. Never been better.

                              MURRAY
                    Stanley-

                              BREE
                    Bree! Sabrina. Claire. Osborne.

Elizabeth comes in, pausing in the doorway. Her face is
streaked with tears. She clutches Lucky to her breast.

                              MURRAY
                    You're going to have to give us
                    more time with that. Your mother
                    and I both love you--

                              ELIZABETH
                    But we don't respect you! I'll
                    never understand how you could do
                    this to me.

                              BREE
                    I'm not doing anything to you! I'm
                    gender dysphoric. It's a genetic
                    condition.

                              ELIZABETH
                    Don't try to blame your father and
                    me for this. You shouldn't use so
                    much mayonnaise. Are you trying to
                    give yourself a heart attack? Let
                    me do that.

She pushes Bree aside, takes over fixing the sandwiches.

ELIZABETH (CONT'D)
Do you know what I see when I look
at you? I see a lost soul crying
out for help. This would never have
happened if you had only come to
church when you were little,
instead of going off to that
synagogue of your father's.

Sydney comes into the kitchen.

SYDNEY
Mom, Dad, there's a sort of scruffy
looking kid outside-
     (seeing Bree)
Holy shit.

ELIZABETH
Language, Sydney!

SYDNEY
I don't fucking believe it.
Stanley.

BREE
Bree.

SYDNEY
Bree. Well, Bree, I was hoping
you'd show up one of these days,
take some of the heat off me.

BREE
It's nice to see you too.

SYDNEY
If that kid out there's your
boyfriend, I'm going to slit my
wrists.

BREE
I need to talk to you in private.

SYDNEY
Oh my God - he is. You lucky son of
a-- I mean, you lucky bitch.

ELIZABETH
Your boyfriend?? That filthy
teenage juvenile delinquent who
came to the door?

                    BREE
He happens to be a very clean,
healthy and respectable young man.

                    ELIZABETH
I don't want to hear any more about
it. How old is he?

                    BREE
Seventeen.

                    ELIZABETH
Oh my God, Murray, he's underage.

                    BREE
Mom, he's my son.

                    ELIZABETH
We should never have spent all that
money sending you to all those
colleges for so many years. That's
where you came under the influence
of those long haired humanists!

                    BREE
He's my son!

                    SYDNEY
You're shitting me.

                    BREE
Remember Emma Wilkins?

                    ELIZABETH
What are you saying?

                    SYDNEY
Is Emma here too?

                    BREE
She killed herself.

                    SYDNEY
Jesus. Kinehora.

                    ELIZABETH
Are you trying to tell me that boy
who came to the door-

                    BREE
He's your grandson.

> ELIZABETH
> Is my grandson. My grandson? Dear
> God.

> BREE
> He doesn't know anything and I
> don't want him to.

Elizabeth rushes out of the room. Bree hurries after her.

> MURRRAY
> Call me Grandpa.

Murray and Sydney follow Elizabeth and Bree.

112   EXT. PHOENIX HOUSE - DAY   112

Elizabeth rushes up to Toby, who's taken aback by her sudden
overwhelming presence.

> ELIZABETH
> You poor thing. Get up off of that
> filthy ground. There could be all
> kinds of awful things down there.
> Look at you. Such a handsome boy.
> Do you know who I am? I'm your--

Bree rushes up and gets between Elizabeth and Toby.

> BREE
> Your friend Bree's mother. Excuse
> us a minute.

She drags Elizabeth off and furiously whispers in her ear.
Sydney and Murray arrive on the scene.

> SYDNEY
> Hi there. I'm Sydney.

> TOBY
> Toby.

> MURRAY
>   (offering his hand)
> Whadayasay?

> ELIZABETH
> Toby, come inside where it's air
> conditioned and I'll fix you up a
> nice big plate of food.

113   INT. PHOENIX KITCHEN - DAY   113

The family sits around the table, watching Toby eat. Sydney takes a bite of casserole from Toby's picked-over plate.

                    SYDNEY
          Mmm, defrosted to perfection.

                    ELIZABETH
          Finish your vegetables.

                    BREE
          He doesn't like broccoli.

                    ELIZABETH
          Open up.

Elizabeth spears a bite of broccoli, holds it up to Toby's mouth. Toby makes a face, but lets her feed him the broccoli. Elizabeth sees Lucky licking his crotch.

                    ELIZABETH (CONT'D)
          Lucky, no! I swear that dog's a sex
          maniac. Just like your father.

                    MURRAY
          At least he gets more action than I
          do.

                    TOBY
          My mom used to live in Phoenix,
          before I was born.

                    BREE
          Really? What a coincidence.

                    TOBY
          What'd your name used to be, when
          you were a guy?

A moment of silence.

                    ELIZABETH
          Honey, why don't you go watch TV in
          the guest bedroom?

                    BREE
          You can take the dog.

                    TOBY
          C'mon, Lucky! Come here, boy!

He goes out of the room with Lucky on his heels.

                    ELIZABETH
          Stanley, what are you planning to
          do with that poor boy?

                    BREE
          Well first of all, I'm going to
          make sure he knows that he's
          encouraged and supported. And that
          he's respected. And maybe even-
          Well at least that he's respected.

114   INT. ELIZABETH'S CLOSET - NIGHT   114

Bree rifles through the colorful outfits in Elizabeth's walk-
in closet. Sydney comes to the doorway.

                    SYDNEY
          Behold the return of the prodigal
          son.
             (off Bree's look)
          So - Bree. Is that like the cheese?

                    BREE
          Could we try to be nice to each
          other? Please?

                    SYDNEY
          This is so bizarre. I can still see
          Stanley in you, but it's like you
          put yourself through a strainer and
          got rid of all the boy pulp.

Bree holds one of her mother's pieces of resort fashionwear
up to herself.

                    SYDNEY (CONT'D)
          Planning a game of bridge with the
          girls?

                    BREE
          Can I borrow a thousand dollars?

                    SYDNEY
          You've got to be kidding.

                    BREE
          Five hundred? Two-hundred fifty?

                    SYDNEY
        Do I hear a dollar and a half? I've
        got to account for every penny.
        Eighteen months sober and they're
        still scared shitless I'm going to
        relapse and wind up passed out on
        the floor in some dive down on Van
        Buren. God, those were the days.

                    BREE
        My surgery's the day after
        tomorrow. I need airfare to get
        home.

                    SYDNEY
        Jeez. You know, growing up I always
        thought you were the lucky one.

                    BREE
        Because I wasn't adopted?

                    SYDNEY
        Yeah. It was always so much easier
        for you to disappoint them.

She takes down an over-the-top feathered cocktail dress.

                    SYDNEY (CONT'D)
        Try this one.

                    BREE
        Oh my God.

                    SYDNEY
        It'll be like showgirls meets the
        ice capades.

                    BREE
        I'm a transsexual, not a
        transvestite.

                    SYDNEY
        But it'll really freak Mom out.

                    BREE
        Now you've lost all credibility.

115   INT. ELIZABETH'S BATHROOM - NIGHT   115

Bree applies her mother's make-up. She gets an idea. She
opens the medicine cabinet, finds a bottle of hormone pills:
her mother's Premarin. She swallows one of them. Then she
grabs a kleenex, tips out more pills for safe-keeping.

116   INT. PHOENIX LIVING ROOM - NIGHT   116

Everyone's there except Bree. Toby, wearing clean clothes of
"80's" vintage, toys with a statue of a penguin on skis made
of bananas. Elizabeth holds Lucky. Murray brings her a
cocktail.

                    ELIZABETH
          Don't break that, Toby. It's very
          expensive. Murray, I hate the way
          you had Lucky's tail clipped. It
          stands straight up like that, just
          like a penis.

                    MURRAY
          Black and hairy?

                    ELIZABETH
          Well, it does.

                    SYDNEY
          Not like any penis I've ever seen.

                    TOBY
          Me neither.

                    ELIZABETH
          Toby! Toby, come here, honey. Let
          me fix your hair. Come on. Come on,
          honey.

Toby rolls his eyes, but she's an irresistable force. He
walks over to her.

                    ELIZABETH (CONT'D)
          Sit.
               (to Lucky)
          Stay. Ha ha.
               (brushing Toby's hair)
          You have such nice thick hair, just
          like mine. And those clothes make a
          world of difference.

                         TOBY
                They fit good, huh?

                         ELIZABETH
                They fit *well*.

                         SYDNEY
                Grammar police.

                         BREE (O.S.)
                Good evening.

Everyone turns. Bree stands at the doorway to the living
room. She's wearing a flowing pink dress, her mother's make-
up - which isn't the right shade for her complexion - and an
artificial flower in her hair. She glides into the room as
gracefully as she can.

                         ELIZABETH
                That dress looks perfectly
                ridiculous.

Ignoring her mother, Bree sits, turns to Toby.

                         BREE
                You're looking very handsome.

                         TOBY
                You look good too.

                         ELIZABETH
                Beauty is relative.

                         SYDNEY
                For God's sake, Mom.

                         ELIZABETH
                Oh, don't pick on me, not tonight.
                I can't take it.

117   INT. PHOENIX RESTAURANT - NIGHT   117

The family follows a HOSTESS to a table. Murray walks with
his arm around Toby.

                         MURRAY
                Never read pornography in the
                toilet. I used to read pornography
                in the toilet and ever since I've
                had shitty sex. You get it?

Toby nods and laughs. Elizabeth stands beside her chair, looks pointedly at Bree. Bree shakes her head. Elizabeth nods. And Bree, like the son she used to be, pulls Elizabeth's chair back for her. The only seat left is at Elizabeth's side. Bree starts to sit.

> ELIZABETH
> Toby, come and sit here next to me.
> (handing Bree a camera)
> Take a picture. Murray, scoot over.
> Toby, honey, lean in close. All
> right, one, two-

Bree snaps the photo. A LADY smiles at the family scene. Sydney grins at her.

> SYDNEY
> We all look much happier than we
> really are.

> TOBY
> Could we get one of us two?

> SYDNEY
> I'll take it.

Toby goes to stand beside Bree. He awkwardly puts an arm around her. Sydney snaps the picture. Toby holds Bree's chair for her.

> LADY
> It's so nice to see a young man
> being so polite to his mother.

> ELIZABETH
> That's not his mother.

118   INT. PHOENIX RESTAURANT - NIGHT   118

The WAITER brings their food. Toby clasps his hands in prayer, eyes Bree expectantly. Bree shakes her head. Elizabeth follows their silent exchange.

> ELIZABETH
> Toby, do you want to say grace? Go
> ahead, honey. Don't be shy.

She clasps her hands and lowers her head. Murray rolls his eyes. Everyone looks at Toby. He feels like a deer caught in the headlights.

                    TOBY
          God bless this restaurant, and
          these thy gifts which we are about
          to receive, forever and ever.

                    ELIZABETH
          And thank you, Lord, for bringing
          Toby to us.

Murray takes a bite of food.

                    ELIZABETH (CONT'D)
          And please let us all stay together
          in health and spirits, in Jesus
          Christ's name, Amen.

                    BREE
          Amen.

                    SYDNEY
          Shalom Yisrael.

Murray coughs, spits a toothpick out of his mouth.

                    MURRAY
          Jesus Christ. You know what's good?
          I'll tell you what's good. This
          toothpick I just ate.

                    ELIZABETH
          Toby, honey, don't take the lettuce
          off of your hamburger - it's good
          for you. Sydney - don't play with
          your food.

                    SYDNEY
          Seig heil.

                    BREE
          Can I borrow a thousand dollars?

                    ELIZABETH
          Toby, your hamburger's almost raw.
          Let me send it back.

                    BREE
          I can pay it back. With interest.

                    MURRAY
          What's the money for?

                    BREE
          To get back to Los Angeles.

                    ELIZABETH
          Look at your life. You've never
          been able to stick to a decision.
          Ten years of college, not a single
          degree. How do you know you're not
          going to change your mind about
          this, too?

                      BREE
          Because I know.

                    ELIZABETH
          Don't do this awful thing to
          yourself. Please. I miss my son.

                      BREE
          Mom, you never had a son.

                    ELIZABETH
          How can you say such a thing? This
          is tearing me apart.

                      BREE
          Now you know how I felt when you
          hired those private detectives.

                    ELIZABETH
          We only tried to do what was best
          for you.

                      BREE
          Is that why you tried to have me
          committed?

                    ELIZABETH
          You tried to kill yourself!

                      BREE
          Because you tried to have me
          committed!

                    ELIZABETH
          I don't know why you always get so
          emotional!

                      BREE
          I am not emotional!!
               (beat; gaining control of herself)
          Oh, God. My cycle's all out of
          whack.

                    ELIZABETH
          You don't have cycles!

> BREE
> Hormones are hormones. Yours and
> mine just happen to come in little
> purple pills.

> ELIZABETH
> (to the Waiter)
> Young man, can we have some doggie
> bags here? I'm going to finish
> cooking his hamburger at home.

> MURRAY
> The toothpick was delicious. After
> the toothpick everything was all
> downhill.

119   INT. PHOENIX KITCHEN - NIGHT   119

The family files into the house.

> ELIZABETH
> Murray, give me your wallet.
> (to Bree)
> Here's two hundred dollars. We'll
> get the rest out of the safe.

Bree reaches her hand out. Elizabeth snatches the money away.

> ELIZABETH (CONT'D)
> There's one condition. I want Toby
> to stay here with us.
> (to Toby)
> Wouldn't you like that, honey? You
> can have your own little apartment.
> We'll remodel the guest house. Do
> you play tennis? We have eight new
> courts at the country club. Murray
> and I just think you ought to have
> a stable, loving family with the
> means to give you every chance that
> you deserve.

Toby stares at Elizabeth, not knowing what to think.

120   EXT. PHOENIX HOUSE - NIGHT   120

Toby dog paddles in the lit-up turquoise pool.

121   INT. SYDNEY'S ROOM - NIGHT   121

Bree stands staring out the window. Elizabeth comes outside to bring Toby an inflatable pool toy. She laughs and encourages him as he plays in the water.

122   EXT. PHOENIX HOUSE - NIGHT   122

Toby lies on a patio lounger. Bree comes out to join him.

> BREE
> Half Italian villa, half country club. How could they spend so much money to make something so...

> TOBY
> Ersatz?

> BREE
> Ersatz. Very good.

Toby looks around at the brightly lit water, the surreal shadows of palm fronds thrown by the garden lighting.

> TOBY
> "Beauty is relative."

> BREE
> Not my relatives.

> TOBY
> No shit.

> BREE
> You don't like my relatives?
>   (off Toby's shrug)
> I wish just once they'd look at me and see me. That's all. Just really see me.

> TOBY
> Why are they trying to be so nice to me?

Bree can't find an answer to this. She shakes her head.

> TOBY (CONT'D)
> Do you think I ought to stay here?

> BREE
> Do you want to?

                    TOBY
          Well, it's pretty nice.

                    BREE
          I think you ought to do whatever
          you think is best for you. But if
          you want, you can come and live
          with me. I can't give you anything
          like this, but I'm sure we can
          manage something.

                    TOBY
          Did you really try to kill
          yourself?

                    BREE
          I swallowed half a bottle of
          Nembutal. Then I panicked and
          called 911.

                    TOBY
          Maybe you're not the suicidal type.

                    BREE
          Maybe. Or maybe my mother's right
          and I just can't stick to a
          decision.

Toby looks at her uneasily.

123   INT. SYDNEY'S ROOM - NIGHT   123

Bree sits in bed, flipping through an old photo album.
There's a knock. Toby comes in. Bree shuts the album.

                    BREE
          Can't you sleep?

                    TOBY
          Not really.

                    BREE
          Do you need something? A glass of
          milk?

                    TOBY
          No.

                    BREE
          What is it? I must look awful.

                    TOBY
          You look good. You look well.

He sits on the bed, takes her hand.

                    BREE
          Don't worry.

Suddenly Toby presses his lips to Bree's in a kiss. Bree is
so hungry for physical affection that for the briefest second
she allows it to happen. Then she recoils.

                    BREE (CONT'D)
          Mmm- What are you doing?

                    TOBY
          What I'm good at.

He shrugs out of his robe.

                    BREE
          Oh, no. No, no.

                    TOBY
          It's okay. I want to. You'll like
          it. I promise.

                    BREE
          I don't want to like it. I don't
          want it at all.

                    TOBY
               (hurt)
          Okay.

He turns away from her.

                    TOBY (CONT'D)
          I'll marry you if you want. I don't
          care how big your place is. I just
          want to be with you. I think you're
          sexy Bree. It's like- Like I see
          you.

                    BREE
          Oh, God.

Toby stands, drops his robe, moves toward her again.

                    BREE (CONT'D)
          No! Put your clothes on, I mean it,
          right now!

                    TOBY
          What's the matter?

                    BREE
          Can you please just cover yourself
          up?

Toby grabs his fallen robe, wraps it around his hips, sits.

                    BREE (CONT'D)
          I am such a total shit.

                    TOBY
          No you're not.

                    BREE
          There's something I should have
          told you a long time ago. You're
          going to hate me.

                    TOBY
          What?

                    BREE
          I'm not really exactly...affiliated
          with a church.

                    TOBY
          I already figured that out.

Bree opens the photo album, points to a snapshot of herself
when she was Stanley with Emma, Toby's mother.

                    TOBY (CONT'D)
          It's my mom and dad.

                    BREE
          It's your mom and me. Toby, I'm so
          sorry. I know I shouldn't have lied
          to you. I know how disappointed you
          must be. A one-bedroom apartment
          instead of a mansion, half Jewish
          instead of half Indian. Toby-

Toby abruptly stands and makes a beeline for the door. Bree
hurries after him as he walks quickly back to his room.

                    BREE (CONT'D)
          Why don't we try to look on the
          bright side? We've gotten to know
          each other, our strengths and
          weaknesses, and we're still good
          friends, aren't we? I'm so sorry.
                    (MORE)

                    BREE (CONT'D)
          I really, truly didn't mean to hurt
          you. My mother's probably right.
          I'm a terrible influence. Oh
          please, this is a terrible time for
          me, I should be-

As Toby's about to disappear into his room she grabs his arm.

                    BREE (CONT'D)
          Toby, wait!

Toby spins and SLUGS her. She falls to the ground.

                    TOBY
          You are not my father!

Toby disappears into his room. Elizabeth and Sydney, who have
been watching from a doorway, hurry to Bree's side. Elizabeth
strokes Bree's head.   ,

                    ELIZABETH
          It's all right. He didn't mean any
          harm, honey. He's just a little bit
          upset.

124   INT. TOBY'S ROOM - NIGHT   124

Toby sits on his bed, head in his hands, panting, trying not
to cry.

125   EXT. GOLF COURSE- DAY   125

Sprinklers circle over the lush fairways. Dawn is breaking.

126   INT. ELIZABETH'S BATHROOM - DAY   126

Bree carefully applies make-up to camouflage the bruise on
her face. Elizabeth and Sydney rush in.

                    SYDNEY
          Toby's gone.

                    ELIZABETH
          He took my purse. And my bucking
          bronco statue.

Bree stares at them, paralyzed.

                    ELIZABETH (CONT'D)
          What do you want to do, Stan-

                         SYDNEY
          Bree.

Elizabeth nods mutely. Bree stares into the mirror, thinking.

127   EXT. PHOENIX HOUSE - DAY   127

Bree stands with a COP, filing a missing persons report.

                         COP
          He's seventeen but you don't know
          his date of birth? What's your
          relationship to the missing boy?

                         BREE
               (beat; then resolutely-)
          I am his father. Can't you put out
          an APB or something?

                         COP
          We'll do our best. I'm sorry to say
          this, but chances are if he doesn't
          want to be found, he's going to
          stay lost.

128   EXT. PHOENIX HOUSE - DAY   128

Bree's family sees her into an airport van.

129   HOSPITAL MONTAGE - DAY/NIGHT   129

--Bree walks slowly down a long, lonely hospital corridor.

--Margaret waits in the admissions office. Bree comes to the
doorway. Margaret stands, greets her with a hug.

--An ORDERLY wheels Bree, who is prepped for surgery, down a
hallway on a hospital gurney.

                         BREE
          Thank you very much.

--Bree lies in a hospital bed, drawn and haggard. A NURSE
checks her IV and catheter.

                         NURSE
          Everything's fine. The surgery was
          a complete success.

Bree sleepily feels the big bumpy bandage over her groin.

130   INT. HOSPITAL ROOM - DAY   130

Clutching her I.V. stand for support, Bree painfully limps to
the dresser. She opens a drawer, takes out the Christian cap
Toby gave her. She limps back to bed. Margaret comes in.

                    MARGARET
          Hello, my lady. How are you
          feeling? And don't say "like a new
          woman."

                    BREE
          I feel like a medieval heretic
          who's been impaled on a very large
          and very thick stake. With
          splinters.

                    MARGARET
          Nice hat.

                    BREE
          It was a present.

                    MARGARET
          Bree, why do I get the feeling that
          there's something not quite right?
          Last week you said this was going
          to be the happiest day of your
          life.

                    BREE
          Last week was a long time ago.

                    MARGARET
          Talk to me.

                    BREE
            (a long beat)
          I fucked up.

Margaret sits beside her on the bed. She touches Bree's arm.
That's all it takes. Bree's self control melts before our
eyes. Her shoulders shake. Tears leak out of her eyes. She
begins to sob.

                    BREE (CONT'D)
          It hurts.

                    MARGARET
          Oh, honey. That's what hearts do.

Bree's crying is cathartic. She cries for herself, for Toby, for a lifetime of disappointments and lost opportunities. She's in pain, but Margaret understands that every tear is a victory: the walls around Bree's heart have cracked wide open.

131   EXT. BEACH - DAY   131

Toby sits by himself on the beach. Behind him, surfers surf, friends play in the waves. Toby snorts the last of his heroin, throws away the bag. He watches a seagull fly off.

132   INT. BREE'S BATHROOM - DAY   132

Bree luxuriates in a hot tub. She looks great. She touches her new vagina. She smiles.

133   INT. MEXICAN RESTAURANT - DAY   133

Christmas decorations festoon the ceiling and walls. Bree serves coffee to customers - she's been promoted to waitress. Fernando, the cook, launches into a flirtatious Spanish lesson.

> FERNANDO
> Amo la comida Mexicana.

> BREE
> Amo la comida Mexicana.

> FERNANDO
> Y amo a Fernando.

> BREE
> Y amo la comida Mexicana.

134   INT. SCHOOL LIBRARY - DAY   134

A blond teenager in surfer clothes sits at a desk, doing homework. WAYNE, a hunky student, walks up.

> WAYNE
> Library closes in fifteen minutes.

The teenager looks up. It's Toby, with a cheap dye job.

> TOBY
> Wayne, this is really hard. Do you
> think you could give me a hand?

                         WAYNE
              Sure - what subject?

Toby stands, pushes down his surfer shorts.

                         TOBY
              Sex education.

Wayne takes off his shirt. He and Toby go into a clinch.

                         MS. SWALLOW (O.S.)
              All right, cut!

PULL BACK TO REVEAL: It's a video porn shoot. MS. SWALLOW, a
busty ex-pornstar, directs the action.

                         MS. SWALLOW (CONT'D)
              Lucky needs help again. Come on,
              let's go, let's go.

A YOUNG MAN runs out and drops to his knees in front of Toby.

                         MS. SWALLOW (CONT'D)
              Did you take your Viagra?

                         TOBY
              Yes, ma'am.

                         MS. SWALLOW
              When's the last time you came?

                         TOBY
              About two hours ago.

                         MS. SWALLOW
              Christ, kid, you've got to focus.
              We're behind schedule. We've got to
              move!

Toby scrunches his eyes in concentration. He winces, looks
down at the Fluffer.

                         TOBY
              Ouch!

135   INT. BREE'S APARTMENT - NIGHT   135

Bree's on the sofa, studying a textbook. She's in loose
fitting clothes, a more comfortable and revealing outfit than
we've ever seen her in. There's a knock. She goes to the
door, opens it. Toby stands outside.

                    BREE
          ...Toby.

                    TOBY
          Don't think I'm fucking forgiving
          you, because I'm not.

                    BREE
          All right.

                    TOBY
          I only came to see if you did it.

                    BREE
          Did what?

                    TOBY
          Got your dick turned inside out.

                    BREE
          Yes. Won't you come in? Just for a
          little while? I have something for
          you.

                    TOBY
          What?

                    BREE
          Please.

Toby hesitates. Caught by curiosity, he grudgingly comes in.

136   INT. BREE'S LIVING ROOM - EVENING   136

Toby looks around.

                    TOBY
          Your parents' place is a lot nicer.

                    BREE
          My parents' place comes with my
          parents.

He spots an artificial Christmas tree on the table.

                    TOBY
          I thought you said we were Jewish.

                    BREE
          Half Jewish. Through my father, so
          it's technically the wrong half.
                    (MORE)

                    BREE (CONT'D)
          And you're only a quarter. The
          wrong quarter.

Bree clears a textbook and papers off the couch.

                    BREE (CONT'D)
          I'm going to finish my degree. I
          thought I'd take up teaching, maybe
          rent a house someplace, someplace
          with a yard.

                    TOBY
          What've you got for me?

                    BREE
          Hang on on a minute. I've missed
          you. Have a seat.

Bree sits on the couch.

                    BREE (CONT'D)
          So how have you been?

                    TOBY
          I've been all right.

Toby takes out a cigarette. Bree gets him an ashtray.

                    BREE
          Would you care to divulge a few
          more details?

                    TOBY
          I'm making a movie.

                    BREE
          You are?

                    TOBY
          I told you I could. They already
          did the advertisement.

He takes a creased up magazine page out of his pocket, hands
it to Bree. She unfolds it. A tacky ad features a HOT SURFER
posing with several half-clothed young men. The title:
"COWABUNGHOLE!"

                    BREE
          "Cowabunghole."

                    TOBY
          That's Dylan Reeves. He's a big
          star.

                    BREE
          And there's you. It's a very nice
          picture. I like your hair.

                    TOBY
          If you want I can get you a
          discount when it comes out.

                    BREE
          Thank you. That's very considerate.

Bree stands, goes into her bedroom.

                    TOBY
          I bought these clothes at the
          Beverly Center. In Beverly Hills.

Bree comes out with Calvin's cowboy hat. She hands it to
Toby. He takes it, looks at it, says nothing.

                    BREE
          Would you like a coke?

                    TOBY
              (beat; testing her)
          I'll take a beer.

                    BREE
          All right.

She heads for the kitchen. Toby puts on the cowboy hat, leans
back, puts his feet up on the table. Bree stops, turns
around.

                    BREE (CONT'D)
          Young man, if you think you can put
          those dirty tennis shoes up on my
          brand new coffee table, you're
          going to have to think again.

Grudgingly, Toby moves his feet off the table. Bree nods and
goes back into the kitchen.

137   EXT. - BREE'S APARTMENT BUILDING - NIGHT   137

Through Bree's open curtains, we see her come back into the
warm glow of the pink living room. She hands Toby a beer. He
can't get it open. Bree takes it, unscrews it for him, hands
it back.

138   --FADE OUT   138

SCENE NOTES

BY DUNCAN TUCKER

Scene 1: I originally intended to begin the movie with shots of Bree getting ready to leave her safe apartment and go out in the world. When I saw this training DVD, produced by Deep Stealth, a company owned by Calpernia Addams and Andrea James, I knew I wanted to use it and wrote it in.

Calpernia (whose life inspired the Showtime movie *A Soldier's Girl*) and Andrea worked with Felicity while she was preparing for the role of Bree. Andrea gives the voice lesson in scene 1; Calpernia plays the fiddle in the Dallas trans party. I'm happy they could participate in the film.

There are only minimal opening credits, as I'm not a fan of them. I like movies to take me right into the story, zero to sixty in as short a time as possible.

Scene 2: Bree dons her battle armor—foundation garments, bra inserts, layers of clothing, and make-up. I always envisioned an African battle chant on the soundtrack here, both to illuminate Bree's esoteric musical taste, and to underscore her personal preparations for battle before going out to face the dangerous world. This early in the film, I wanted music that was exciting and energetic. I've been a fan of the great Miriam Makeba since my third-grade teacher played "The Click Song" to us in class one day. I used to search for her albums in thrift stores. Now most of them have been reissued on CD. "Jo'Linkomo" is a personal favorite of mine.

Scene 4: A wild Frisbee throw knocks Bree's floppy sun hat off her head. This was pure luck. You pray for accidents like this to happen. Felicity stayed in character and scurried back to fetch the fallen hat before hurrying on her way. Note the "Los Angeles Realty" sign. It was the only way we could afford to establish our Los Angeles location.

Scene 6: This was one of the first scenes we shot. When I saw Felicity sitting in the psychiatrist's office as Bree, every nerve taught, so hopeful, so worried, so focused, I knew something special was happening. Before that day the butterflies in my stomach were the size of elephants. After that scene they shrank down to the size of very large water buffaloes.

In the voice-over dialogue with the psychiatrist, we establish that Bree has undergone facial feminization surgery—including a tracheal shave, which eliminates the Adam's apple. Bree still favors scarves, perhaps to hide a scar, perhaps because covering up is her way of life.

Scene 7: We shot this scene with Felicity singing "You are my hormones, my lovely hormones…" to the tune of "You Are My Sunshine." Later we discovered that that song was not public domain, so I wrote new words and Felicity looped them in to the tune of "Loch Lomond" during post.

This and all the scenes in Los Angeles were filmed in Phoenix near the end of the shoot. We shot one take with Bree pulling her pantyhose down to tuck, giving us a glimpse of her penis, in case an early reveal turned out to be more effective than the later one at the side of the road with Toby.

I asked production designer Mark White for a photo of African tribeswomen who had manipulated their soft tissue to achieve beauty—big lips or long necks. I'm intrigued by the way the photo on the wall echoes Bree's own physical transformation, and as an ex-student of anthropology, I'm sure Bree's intrigued, too.

Scene 9: I contemplated including Toby's side of this conversation, with him on a pay phone in a New York City jail, but decided that it'd be more interesting if the audience first met Toby at the same time Bree did.

Scene 11: This scene was shot in a real therapist's office, in Scottsdale, Arizona's Center for Psychological Well-Being.

I wanted Bree's therapist, Margaret, to be everything Bree is not—comfortable in her body, effortlessly feminine, warm, in touch with her heart. Elizabeth Peña, one of my favorite actors, is perfect in the role. Margaret is part therapist, part friend, part gatekeeper to Bree. I think of her as Gandalf to Bree's Frodo. This scene is the springboard for the action of the movie. It was one of the toughest scenes in the movie to write. I had to collapse an hour-long session into about two minutes.

Thanks to Mark White for the vagina-inspired art on the walls.

Scene 13: Bree's voice is a recurring motif in the movie. You could say that metaphorically speaking, the entire movie is about Bree finding her voice. In this scene, slowing down the record, Bree imagines her voice returning to the timbre of a man's.

Scene 14: We stole this shot—no permits. The other people on the steps are whoever happened to be coming in and out of the government building. We did it in about ten minutes. It would've been really cheap if we hadn't gotten a parking ticket. Felicity's walk is priceless.

Scene 15: I've often been asked if the photos of Bree as Stanley are Felicity in drag. They're not. A young man who worked in a bookstore near my apartment in New York City had a facial structure that was startlingly similar to Felicity's and he was kind enough to give us a few hours of his time. Mark White cooked up the driver's license and the party photo with Toby's mom—who we found through our extras casting agent.

Scene 16: Felicity was actually crying during this scene, because she was so moved by seeing the boy who might be her son for the first time. Yet her discomfort and her equivocation (church of the potential father) trumped her tears. Each time I called "cut," I cracked up, and Felicity would get upset because she had no idea how funny she was being.

Scene 17: Shot in the Odessa Coffee Shop in New York City's East Village. I used to eat there all the time. They make great pierogis and borscht.

Duncan Sheik, a friend of mine, generously recorded the American traditional tune "I Am a Pilgrim" for this scene. I thought the words of the song were perfect for Bree and Toby. The song places them as American pilgrims, and its spiritual theme jibes nicely with Bree's pose as a church lady. Dolly Parton was able to refer back to this song in her lyrics for "Travelin' Thru."

Scene 19: Kevin had a problem with one element of this scene: why would Toby take out something as personal as a photo of his real parents to show it to this strange lady? He was right. We noodled about it for about twenty-five minutes and then a crew member came up with the brilliant idea of taping the picture to the wall above his bed.

Scene 20: Chocolate fudge.

Scenes 21 and 22: Bree's side of the conversation was shot in the first week. Margaret's in the last week.

Scene 23: I love Bree touching the door and reacting to the greasy dirt on her hand. Pam Wise and I cut this scene around that moment.

Scene 24: During auditions, I had one young actor who was up for the part of Alex do an improv on his lines. He came up with "cobwebby old stank Christian pussy." Out of the mouths of babes.

Scenes 26 and 27: Bree and Toby begin their journey together. I posed composer David Mansfield a difficult task: I wanted the music (the first score we hear) to include elements of the African sounds we'd already heard in Bree's apartment, a bass beat that evoked Toby's recent urban past, and then to segue into the acoustic American traditional sound that would recur through the rest of their journey. He did a brilliant job. In these scenes Bree and Toby spar for dominance, like two kids playing king of the hill. Each time one of them scores a point, David threw in an African chant or grunt or shout, a sort of musical "gotcha!"

Scene 28: We cut this scene down for pacing reasons. I hated to lose the "coasters" line.

Scene 35: More trimming here for pacing reasons. Hated to lose the cow/bull thing. Dialogue on the road is not very cinematically interesting, and I decided less was more. I was very insistent about keeping in my *Lord of the Rings* tribute, which Kevin Zegers delivers with panache.

Scene 40: Venida Evans as Arletty was spot-on, every take. Arletty is Toby's neighbor, a woman who sometimes baby-sat for him, and to whom he would go for refuge—though she never knew the extent of his problems at home. Her character is named for one of my favorite movie stars, the French actress Arletty, who starred in *Les Enfants du Paradis.* If you look close, Arletty has little Eiffel Tower figures on her tables. Duke Scoppa, our props master, wants to manufacture an Arletty doll that talks when you pull her string. She'll say, "I could get those couple of little hairs out from under your nose in nothing flat," "That ought to keep them from sticking their heads up again," "I don't know you, Bobby Jensen," and "This man's heavy with sin."

Scene 41: My mom ordered the plastic magnifying headgear Arletty wears from some shopping channel a few years ago and never used them. I think they're hilarious. She lent them to me to use as part of Arletty's home electrolysis set.

Scene 43: We got this as a pick-up shot in California a few months after principal photography. It's the kitchen door of a house in the Hollywood Hills.

Scene 44: Bobby Jensen was played by a fine actor with a brilliant name: Raynor Scheine. Poor Raynor was so bruised after we shot the fight scene that he could barely stand up straight. I often feel I should have developed his character more, and given more time to Toby's home life, but I wanted to keep the story flowing forward at a fast pace, and in the end, for better or worse, I decided to just get in and get out of Callicoon as quickly as possible.

Scene 46: Our Japanese distributor wants to reproduce Toby's stuffed monkey and sell it in stores. It's a wonderful, tattered old thing that Duke found in a thrift store.

Scene 50: Powdered baby formula. Kevin was very disappointed.
   A continuity blooper in this scene—in one shot the call sheet is visible in the side pocket of the car door. It was the martini shot (last shot) of the day and no one noticed it.

Scene 52: I didn't end up shooting this dialogue. I realized on the day that I'd rather tell the story with pictures, so instead Bree offers Toby a mint, and he turns away from her without speaking.
   The song here, "There's a New Moon over My Shoulder," is an old tune recorded for us by the great bluegrass singer Larry Sparks. I love the way the upbeat feel of the music contrasts with the anger and frustration Bree and Toby are feeling.

Scene 54: Just before shooting I suggested to Felicity that Bree might tangle her legs in the gas hose. She loved bits of business like this, and could always make them fly. In one take she actually did a pratfall—flat on her butt (see the outtakes on the DVD). It was hilarious, but too comedic for the tone of the movie. The great geezers on the front porch are some very cool Sullivan County locals. All of the first half of the road trip was filmed in and around the Catskill Mountains.

Scene 55: We shot this in a local all-purpose store in the Catskills. I originally wanted to do this in a giant K-Mart type store, but we couldn't afford the location fee. Similarly, and naively, I originally envisioned some of the road scenes to be shot on interstate highways, and one of the truck stop scenes to be in a giant truck stop with a video arcade, big gift shop, showers in the bathrooms. These sorts of locations cost big bucks. This is why so many indie road movies take place on back roads and in small-town diners and motels.

Scene 58: It was raining on and off throughout the evening we shot this. We had to keep running for cover. Felicity and Kevin and Danny and Lynn and I played word games in the car while the rest of the crew and producers held a tarp over their heads and laughed a lot.

On paper the loon imitations looked good, but it was confusing when we watched it in the editing room. So the loon calls bit the dust. Steve Kazmierski stood out in the middle of the lake in hip waders to get the final long shot. That was one of the few times we used a tripod—we couldn't risk him slipping and dropping the camera into the water. Pam Wise added the bullfrog croak, which helped bring out the humor in Bree's plight.

Scene 61: Felicity and Kevin almost got arrested when we started shooting this scene. We were in New Jersey and unwittingly crossed a stoplight from one town, where we were permitted, to another, where we were not. By the time the cops left we'd lost the light. So the first shot of this scene was filmed in New Jersey, and the rest was picked up in upstate New York several days later.

I cut the dog-tooth dialogue for pacing reasons. Bree already knew Bobby Jensen was a bad guy, and her feelings of remorse didn't need to be revisited.

Scene 63: This is another moment when Felicity didn't know she was being simultaneously heartbreaking and hilarious. I would laugh after each take, and she would worry she was doing something wrong. Genius.

Scene 64: There was no phone booth here; our art department built it in the doorway that led to the parking lot. We didn't normally build things, so this was a special treat. I told Mark White I wanted to see a reflection of Toby and Taylor playing the video game as Bree was talking, and that worked out just fine.

Scene 65: Here's another tune I asked Larry Sparks to record here—"Lay My Burden Down," made famous by Mississippi John Hurt. It speaks to what Bree is feeling, and it's a religious song, so it's perfect for Bree's prayer.

Scene 67: I found the "I'm Proud to Be a Christian" hat at a thrift store during a trip to North Carolina a few years ago. I bought it but never had the guts to wear it. So I wrote it into the movie.

Scene 68: Editor Pam Wise came up with this music cue. It really makes the humor and wildness of the moment fly.

Scenes 70 through 73: All the actors at Mary Ellen's house are trans, with the exception of the Lady in Pink (Lynn Laurino), who's an old college friend of mine, the mother of three, a natural comedienne and a great sport. We shot these scenes in her house. She'd powder her face with great dignity and attention, I'd call cut, and the whole crew would crack up because she had giant blotches of white powder all over her nose and cheeks.

Bianca Leigh, who plays Mary Ellen, is an actress and singer who works in New York theater and nightclubs. She's a natural, and every take we shot of her was great. We didn't have time to get the reverse shot of "Justin Duvall" skateboarding, so I had to cut Mary Ellen's line about him. I really wanted to make clear that she had a good relationship with her neighbors, but we just didn't have the luxury of making that happen.

It was very important to me to have a real trans presence in the movie. I wanted to show audiences a glimpse of the variety of transsexual experience. It's interesting that Felicity—even as her lovely self—is not the most delicately built or feminine-looking woman in the room.

It broke my heart that we only had one afternoon to shoot the entire party scene. If I'd had more time and money I would have liked to have let the camera roll on each of these wonderful transpeople, to capture unplanned moments of truth and humanity. The night before we filmed, Felicity and Kevin and I took all our trans actors out for a beer, and we really lit up that New Jersey strip mall burger joint. Calpernia Addams gave us a clog dancing demonstration, Melissa Sklarz lectured us on New York politics, David Harrison read auras, Sandi Alexander's infectious laugh kept us all bubbling along. I remember calling my editor, Pam, at the end of our shooting day, practically in tears, because we'd only been able to capture a tiny fraction of the richness of their lives.

Scene 74: Toby gets high on Bree's nail polish, then tries on her nightgown. He's wondering for a moment if he's trans, too.

The way Bree comes out of the bathroom and Toby's reaction is a moment of screwball comedy. I think of it as a little homage to one of my favorite filmmakers, Preston Sturges. Although on set we also joked about the similarities to the scene where Jack Nicholson sees Diane Keaton in the altogether in *Something's Gotta Give.*

Scenes 75 and 76: No actual possums were harmed in the shooting of this movie. We used fake fur covered with ketchup.

These are the first Arizona-shot scenes to appear in the movie. They were shot outside of Chino Valley, about two hours north of Phoenix. We were careful not to frame any mountains and the landscape looks enough like western Texas to pass. Felicity and Kevin and I referred to these scenes as Bree's and Toby's honeymoon. It's the first time they actually play together. I wanted a wide shot to bookend scene 75 because the wide open spaces resonate with the opening up of Bree's and Toby's relationship.

David Mansfield's score here is beautiful. It has a slow build, then breaks into a lovely fiddle melody. I liked it so much that I asked him to record a slightly slower version for the final act. When Bree cries, thinking of Toby, the honeymoon music reappears as we cut to the shot of him at the California beach.

Scene 78: At the outset I wasn't sure how I was going to shoot this scene. I figured we'd probably do it from behind, or in silhouette, with an arc of urine illuminated by the car's headlights. But as I saw how real Felicity's transformation into Bree was, how complete an illusion we were able to sustain, I realized I wanted to show the truth of Bree's difficult burden.

My producers called a few special effects houses to find out how much it would cost to get a prosthetic penis that could actually urinate. The price tag turned out to be in the neighborhood of $20,000. That was inconceivable for us—we couldn't have afforded a fraction of that. Fortunately, Felicity had "Andy."

Andy was a latex panty stuffer, something drag kings use for verisimilitude. Felicity procured Andy during rehearsals, and used him so that she'd never forget who she was playing. I had Duke in props drill a hole through Andy, attach a plastic tube that led to a hot water bottle. Then Lynn in make-up painted Andy with Felicity's foundation and blush. Some of the crew offered to pose for her, but she swears she was able to bring Andy to life by working purely from memory.

We finished these preparations only about an hour before shooting in the middle of the night in the middle of the Arizona desert in the middle of nowhere. Felicity held Andy up to herself in the bathroom of our run-down trailer. From beyond the door I heard, "Oh my God… Duncan, you'd better get in here." When I took a look I couldn't hold back my own "Oh my God." From a few feet away, in fluorescent light, Andy looked completely and disturbingly real.

About twenty minutes later, as we were lighting the scene, I noticed that Felicity was looking troubled. I asked to speak to her alone—we went behind the half saloon doors in the back of the trailer, about two yards away from everyone else. I told her I would only keep this shot in the cut of the film if it felt honest and important—that I had no interest in including it if it felt exploitative. She said she understood—and then she began to cry.

As a friend I wanted to comfort her. As a director I stood back and shut up and let her feel her emotions. Felicity's empathy for Bree ran so deep that her crying took her by surprise. Seeing her own body with a penis brought the difficulty of Bree's journey home in a profound way. And the prospect of exposing Bree, even to our movie crew, deeply unsettled her.

As we shot the scene my producers kept asking me to do a shoot-around, in case we wanted to re-edit to avoid an NC-17 rating. I didn't want to do it—the scene was that important to me. So what you see in the movie is the only way we shot it.

Scene 84: We shot this scene at the end of the day, and by the time we did the set-ups inside the car we were losing light fast. When we did Felicity's coverage we had to reflect generator-powered lights off of bounce boards to simulate morning sunlight on her face

I had a vivid image of exactly how I wanted the Hitchhiker to look—

dreadlocks, Chinese hat, suspenders, and all. Danny Glicker went through my closet and found an old T-shirt I'd bought years ago when I was traveling in the South Pacific and co-opted it for the wardrobe department. When Felicity first saw the Hitchhiker in costume she came up to me and said, "I never realized till now that the Hitchhiker is a Shakespearean fool!"

Scene 85: Grant Monohon, who plays the Hitchhiker, used the "level-three vegan" line in conversation with me. I asked where he heard it; he said it was just something his roommate occasionally said. Knowing a good line when I heard it, I said, "I'm using it." After the movie was released I was told that it was very close to a line that was used on *The Simpsons.* Though its presence is an accident, I'm happy there's a little homage to *The Simpsons* in *Transamerica.*

Scene 86: D.P. Steve Kazmierski came up with the idea of Bree turning her head to watch the boys run naked into the water. I love hearing ideas from my collaborators, especially when they're better than my own. This little head turn reveals so much about Bree's exile from life, and her longing to be as free with her body as the boys are with theirs.

Scene 87: This was shot at Watson Lake in the Granite Dells outside of Prescott, Arizona. I went to college across the street from these rock formations. We used to clamber over the boulders and pretend we were exploring distant planets. The water was colder than we thought it would be. Kevin and Grant would climb out between takes to get warm. The make-up girls stood by with towels and rubbed them down—one of the perks of their job.

Grant's a daredevil—he was doing flips into the water before we'd had a chance to check out its depth. Scared the shit out of us.

Scene 88: We had to shoot this scene only as a master; we had no time to get coverage. Bree's line, "Is it soothing?" could have been much funnier if I'd been able to cut to a close-up.

Scene 93: Graham Greene and Felicity had instant chemistry. They knew how to play together—like professionals, like kids. Shooting their scenes was a delight, and that shows on-screen.

Scenes 100 and 101: Felicity learned in her research that singing is particularly difficult for some trans women. (Although not for Bianca Leigh, who, as Mary Ellen, does her own vocals when she sings "Home on the Range.") As when she watched Toby and the Hitchhiker skinny-dip, Bree wants to join in, but can't allow herself to. If you watch Felicity closely you'll see that every few bars she sings a hesitant word or two.

Graham had injured his hands and couldn't play the guitar. My brother John sat with him before shooting, while the crew was eating dinner, and they serenaded us with "Beautiful Dreamer" as a country waltz. David Mansfield later did a great job of filling in the guitar track.

I wrote the "That'll put hair on your chest" line in an early draft of the screenplay because it was irresistible. Then I foolishly took it out because I was afraid it would play too broadly. On our first take of the "Beautiful Dreamer" scene, when Felicity started coughing after her second sip of mescal, Graham ad-libbed the line out of the blue. Felicity responded without missing a beat. That taught me that as long as a line—even a joke line—is grounded in a real moment, great actors will make it fly.

Scene 103: Shot in a master, with no cutaways. It takes several tries to get the timing just right on these master shots.

Calvin's demonstration of the various ways of wearing a cowboy hat is something Graham was joking around with off-camera. I liked it and asked him to put it in the movie. I later learned it was a riff on a bit from an old James Garner comedy western—I think it was *Support Your Local Sheriff*. I remember seeing that movie when I was a kid and loving it. I'm not sure even Graham knew where he'd picked that bit up, but I figure Calvin Manygoats might well be a James Garner fan.

Scene 108: The first appearance of the great Fionnula Flanagan, in tan make-up and shimmering turquoise. Fionnula is one of the few actors I know who can play comedy and tragedy at the same moment. She gives a fearless portrait of a woman who sucks up all the emotional oxygen in the room. I know women exactly like Elizabeth Shupak. And yet it was scary to write so vivid a character. Truth is often stranger than fiction. With great courage and compassion, Fionnula brings home a character who in my life experience is utterly real.

Bree's parents' house is actually my mother's house. Some of Fionnula's wardrobe—though not the turquoise pantsuit—came straight out of my mother's closet.

Scene 110: Burt Young generously took on the supporting role of Murray, Bree's father, a man who only wants peace and quiet, and who's learned that letting his trophy wife play out her emotions with minimal interference is the easiest path to take. He walks around all day in pajamas and a straw hat. I imagine he even goes to the store in those clothes.

Scene 111: Carrie Preston as Sydney. She's a joy. Sydney was the problem child to Stanley's perfect little boy. I imagine they didn't get along too well as kids. Although with this visit, things begin to shift.

I cut Fionnula's "long-haired humanists" line for pacing reasons, though she delivered it hilariously.

Scene 113: Zero T. Poodle (The "T" stands for "The") in his big close-up. Zero sat in the director's chair for most of the shoot and took over for me whenever I needed a break. As I write this he's busy figuring out how to get a small ball out of a big cardboard box. He's a problem solver. The grips made him his own grip vest, with pockets, Velcro tape, markers, duct tape, and clothespins—an entire grip toolkit.

His motivation in this scene: peanut butter and honey.

Scene 114: My mom's closet, my mom's clothes.

I made minor trims to the scene in the editing room for pacing reasons. Also, people didn't seem to understand the "it was so much easier for you to disappoint them" line.

Scene 116: A surprisingly large number of people I've met since finishing the film have been fascinated by the penguin on banana skis sculpture. Several have asked if they could buy it. Sorry—it's my mom's.

I wanted the dress Bree makes her appearance in to be one she'd admired in her mother's closet ever since she was a child. Her fairy princess dress. Danny Glicker shopped like crazy to find the right thing. Felicity tried dresses on throughout the shoot, and nothing really perfect had turned up by the day of this scene. Danny ran out to thrift stores that morning and came back with an armload of new possibilities—including this sheer pink number. The moment Felicity put it on, we knew it was exactly right.

Bree wants so badly for her family to see her as a woman instead of as Stanley in a dress. She's wearing her mother's make-up, which is the wrong shade for her complexion, frosted lipstick, and she's found a little artificial flower to ornament her hair. As happens to many of us, being home again has made her take a giant step backward into childhood patterns of self-consciousness.

Scene 117: A restaurant we couldn't afford, donated by Marriott's Camelback Inn. The Marriott Company was thrilled to have Felicity and her husband Bill Macy (who served as executive producer) at their resort, and they helped us out a lot. It probably didn't hurt that we were shooting off-season in Phoenix (120 degrees in the shade), and the place was pretty empty anyway. But they were great, and cut us a fantastic deal for crew accommodations in one of their other resort hotels. So every night the crew had a big pool and hot tub to relax in, tennis courts, tropical cocktails, the works—and morale in Phoenix stayed high.

Scene 118: As Fionnula paints a rosy picture of the life Toby would have with them, she closes the metal security shutters like a trap.

Scene 123: Before shooting this scene I was very concerned about performance, because there's so much going on here, and it's so delicately balanced between sweetness, sadness, shame, embarrassment, sexiness, and humor. But Felicity and Kevin nailed it.

Bree's so starved for affection she allows him to kiss her for nearly a second before breaking away. When The Weinstein Company did test screenings in Manhattan and in the suburbs of New Jersey, several Manhattan audience members said, "This scene made me uncomfortable. I loved it." Interestingly, several suburban audience members said, "This scene made me uncomfortable. I didn't like it."

Scene 127: Another scene we had to pick up in Los Angeles a few months after the end of principal photography. We just didn't have time for it in Phoenix. I tried to cut around this scene, but it was too important to see the moment when Bree stands tall and says, "I am his father."

Scenes 130, 131, 132: Margaret understands that Bree's crying is a kind of victory. The self-protective walls around her heart have cracked open.

I think of these as the water scenes. First, Bree melts—liquefies—before our eyes. Then Toby reaches the end of his journey at the Pacific Ocean. (Filmed in Malibu; I'd never seen the southern California Pacific look more blue.) And finally, Bree emerges from the water in her bathtub like Venus from the surf. Or like someone newly baptized—a classic symbol of rebirth.

The shot of Toby at the beach was also picked up in Los Angeles, which I guess is obvious. Kevin had cut his hair and dyed it to get the bad peroxide blond out, and if you look close, you'll see his hair doesn't quite match the way it looked in the rest of the movie.

Someone told me that some critic somewhere actually thought Bree was masturbating in the bathtub. That wasn't my intention in this scene, but I suppose as an interpretation, masturbation isn't uninteresting.

Scene 134: Shot in my mom's garage. The porn shoot crew are *Transamerica* crew members.

Our great sound editor, Lou Bertini, supplied me with a muffled "sorry" after Toby winces and says "Ouch!" to the fluffer who's working on him. It was pretty funny, and I find it hard to resist a gag, but ultimately it interfered with the emotional flow of the scene.

Scene 136: Bree wears looser, lighter, and more revealing clothes than she ever has before. It was a complete accident that her pants match her couch, but I love it.

Mark White created the "Cowabunghole" advertisement. He did a great job and I can only imagine the hours of research time he must have put in. Several of our crew members, and maybe even one producer, posed for him and became instant porn legends.

In the first draft I wrote that Bree gave Toby the stuffed monkey toy she'd rescued from his stepfather's garage. Later I realized that was too infantile an image and changed it to Calvin's hat.

No one ever notices, but the snapshot that Bree's sister Sydney took of Bree and Toby sits framed on the coffee table beside the sofa.

Scene 137: Some audiences seem to catch on that Toby can't open his beer bottle and Bree opens it for him, and some audiences don't. That's fine by me. I like that Bree's not pretending anymore, and that the moment's not forced.

★　★　★

On "Travelin' Thru" by Dolly Parton

A few months before the movie opened in New York and Los Angeles I had the idea of asking Dolly Parton to write a song for the end credits. She's a living symbol of self-invention, life force, family values, and love without judgment—all of which are themes of *Transamerica*. She's also a brilliant singer and songwriter.

I asked my agents at William Morris (by this time I had agents) if we could get a copy of the movie to Dolly's office. George Freeman and Joel Roman made a few calls and a DVD was overnighted to her. That was the last I expected to hear about it.

And then several days later the phone rang. Dolly liked the movie and wanted to write a song. I e-mailed her a long letter—I said I envisioned a song about a pilgrim on a journey, a song with a traditional revival-camp feel, a tune you could snap your fingers to, one that could be sung in dance halls as well as in churches.

A few weeks later the phone rang again. Dolly had written a song. When the call came I was in Detroit at a film festival. Extraordinarily, Dolly was in Detroit for one day to do a concert. I had an hour off between press interviews and the screening—between 4 and 5 P.M. Dolly had one hour off between rehearsal and sound check—between 4 and 5 P.M. So on our free hour I was driven to the back lot of the Fox Theater in downtown Detroit and shown to her purple tour bus. Dolly was sitting inside, looking great in black leather, practicing the song with her guitar.

She jumped up, took my coat, got me some water, and made sure I was comfortable. And then she sang the song for me. I liked it immediately.

I asked her about shifting a verse here, a chorus there, what she thought about adding a slow a capella section. Not all my ideas worked—but every time I offered one, she said, "Let's try it!" She was game for anything and a pleasure from the first moment I met her.

At the end of our hour together she checked her schedule and said she could detour her tour bus to Nashville the following week for one day to lay down the song. She asked if I'd like to come to be in the studio with her to help out. I would've walked to Nashville if I had to.

Working with Dolly and her superb musicians was one of the highlights of my year. Dolly worked harder than anyone—she was up with me until about 2 A.M, well after the musicians had gone home, laying down background vocals and harmonies. Our goal was for the song to sound as down-home and homemade as possible, to let Dolly's voice soar in the foreground, with a rootsy acoustic interplay of strings and hand-drumming in the background. We incorporated a motif of African-sounding back-up chants, so that "Travelin' Thru" acts as a bookend with Miriam Makeba's African battle song "Jo'Linkomo," which is heard at the beginning of the movie.

I think "Travelin' Thru" is as strong as anything Dolly's ever written, and she sings the hell out of it. She's a force of nature and a source of joy, and I'll always be grateful to her, to my agents, and to providence that she became part of *Transamerica*.

STILLS

Toby (Kevin Zegers) and Bree (Felicity Huffman) snapped by Sydney (Carrie Preston) in the Phoenix restaurant.

Bree strides forth to do battle. Her costumes, a combination of camouflage and
battle armor, were created by Danny Glicker.

Bree at home.

Bree sees Toby for the first time.

Kevin Zegers freezing his butt off: "You're not a freak. You're just a liar."

"Welcome to the first meeting of the Gender Pride Presidents Day Weekend Caribbean Cruise Planning Committee." —Bianca Leigh as Mary Ellen

"Here are some arrowheads. They're only $1.50 each."

"Just because a person doesn't go around blabbing her entire biological history to everyone she meets doesn't make her a liar."

Costume design by
Danny Glicker

Polyester clothes and pancake make-up: a must for summer in the desert.

Comedy and tragedy in the same face.

Kevin and Felicity react in character to Graham Greene improvising at the end of a take—he's talking about one of his brothers running a whorehouse.

Graham Greene (as Calvin Manygoats) in a rare good–humored moment.

Beautiful Dreamers.

Watching Calvin on Storm Ranch: "Do my breasts look smaller to you?"

Calvin bids Bree farewell.

Bree watches Calvin drive off into the sunset.

Burt Young as Murray, Fionnula Flanagan as Elizabeth, and Zero T. Poodle as Lucky.

"What a handsome boy."

"Planning a game of bridge with the girls?"

The long, lonely walk. We placed the camera low so Felicity would look tall.

Bree comes home: liquefaction and victory.

Last day of shooting—Felicity between takes.

Duncan Tucker relaxing on the beach.

The crew daringly hand-carried the camera over slippery rocks to Backflip Island.

Shooting in northern Arizona. We were locked out of the light truck that day.

Felicity and ace sound recorder Griffin Richardson.

Kevin Zegers and a girl he picked up.

Griffin Richardson, Felicity Huffman, Rebecca Fulton, Duncan ("No Sniveling") Tucker, and Sebastian ("Hogs in Heat") Dungan discuss metaphysics on the last day of shooting.

Fionnula Flanagan and Duncan Tucker take a well-deserved break.

Bree leaves home to confront the psychiatrist. Shot on the last day of principal
photography. Steve Kazmierski holds the camera.

It took three tries to get Kevin's dye
job to look this cheap.

Toby becomes a movie star.

Top: Director Duncan Tucker wearing his brother's cowboy hat, on loan for the
   Arizona desert portion of the shoot.

Bottom: Producer Linda Moran and Kevin Zegers play strip Ping–Pong at dawn at
   the hotel after the last day of shooting.

Some of the cast and crew got together to toast the end of principal photography, and kept toasting until dawn.

TRANSFORMATION

FROM FELICITY TO BREE

Would Bree watch *Desperate Housewives?* Yes, she would love it and throw *Desperate Housewives* parties. She might even consider going blonde.
                                                                    —*Felicity Huffman*

Huffman is that rare gifted actor who has demonstrated not only great range but also a fierce sense of independence in the roles she has chosen and created onstage and on the small and big screens.

Huffman is, after all, co-founder, with William H. Macy and David Mamet, of New York's Atlantic Theatre Company. She has been nominated for numerous Golden Globe and Emmy awards for the tough women she has created on the acclaimed TV series *Sports Night* and *Desperate Housewives.* And she has done memorable supporting work in such acclaimed films as *The Spanish Prisoner* and *Magnolia.*

But with *Transamerica,* Huffman, for the first time, carries an entire feature film. Her portrayal of Bree, a conservative, biologically male transsexual "living stealth" in the days before her scheduled surgery, is a triumph of transformation, an astonishing example of how completely an actor can fearlessly disappear into the skin, and psyche, of another person.

Transamerica opens with startling sound and image: an attractive woman, looking right into the camera, modulates her voice from high to low. In a moment we realize this is a training video that Bree is watching, an exercise that is helping her more fully become a woman.

The opening also invites the audience to witness the transformation of a star of a wildly popular TV series into an almost unrecognizable character whose greatest desire is to avoid the notice of others.

The film's writer-director, Duncan Tucker, says, "*Transamerica* is subversive insofar as the main character is a transsexual woman, yet the film is not about transsexuality. It is at root an old-fashioned story about a parent, a child and the bonds of family."

131

Huffman, who learned about Tucker's offer for her to star in *Transamerica* while she was at the first table read for the *Desperate Housewives* pilot, adds that "Duncan told me, 'It's not a movie about what's under your skirt.'"

Creating Bree, says Huffman, was about getting across the idea "that you feel alienated from your true being, that you feel you are an impostor."

Did Huffman feel that taking the role was a risk?

"Risky, no, scary, yes," she admits. "I didn't think I could pull it off. I knew nothing about the transgender world. How does a woman go about becoming a man who is becoming a woman? Did I become a man first and then figure out how, as a man, I should let my inner woman out?"

Says producer Sebastian Dungan, "I think Felicity was fearless in playing Bree because there is always a risk of being perceived differently or typecast when you play a role like Bree. But," he continues, "I also believe Felicity, as an artist, is dedicated to honesty and, as a person, loves a challenge. So, I don't think she was worried about perception or glamour. She just saw a great part and dove into it."

Adds Huffman, "Everyone has had experiences like the ones Bree has: being self-conscious on an excruciating level, not fitting in, wishing people could see you as you really are, having to hide your true self from those you love. True gender-dysphoric individuals experience this at an intense level, but it is still a truth of the human soul. If *Transamerica* can tell a story about that, it transforms it from an 'issue movie' to a movie everyone can relate to because the characters' struggles are true and universal. And those are the movies I want to watch."

★ ★ ★

The makers of *Transamerica* had very firm ideas about the kind of actor they wanted for Bree.

"The casting of Bree was always one of the trickiest parts of putting together the film," recalls Dungan. "Many people suggested we cast a male actor, but the last thing we wanted was for Bree to look like a man in women's clothes. We felt it would be too difficult to make a man pass completely as a transsexual woman without costly and cumbersome prosthetics and makeup."

Although Bree would be played by a woman, Huffman nonetheless went through a radical physical as well as emotional transformation to prepare for the part.

"I had to figure out the physicality of the role," she recalls. "I met with two wonderful women, Andrea James and Calpernia Addams [on whose life the award-winning Showtime movie *A Soldier's Girl* was based]. They talked to me not only about the inner life of gender dysphoria but about the physical challenges. They were my guardian angels throughout the shooting.

"I remember Danny Glicker, the brilliant costume designer, and I calling Andrea, asking, 'What does it feel like right after sexual reassignment surgery and what does the bandage look like?' We passed the phone back and forth as she described the bandage to him and the pain to me."

Adds Tucker, "We often think of all TS women as odd-looking, caught in a limbo between masculine and feminine. That is because we're often only aware of the visible ones, the TS people we recognize on the street. In fact, every year hundreds of 'stealth trannies' pass through transition and then melt invisibly into society."

To reach a point where Bree could look, sound, walk, talk, and dress like a transgender person who is on the verge of successfully "living stealth," at least most of the time, Huffman and the *Transamerica* crew worked diligently on the most extreme of makeovers.

Huffman began by asking herself, "How *does* a woman stand, sit, gesture?"

Says Huffman, "I went to work with a wonderful coach, Danea Doyle, who teaches transgender woman how to behave like women. I had to learn everything from the outside in. I learned how to walk, how to hold my arms and hands. For example, men's arms are longer and their hands are much bigger, so to hide this I stood with my elbows severely tucked in and my hands neatly folded over each other. I learned how to stand, walk, and gesture. For me, interestingly enough, a large part of the transformation was training to be more feminine."

Huffman continues, "For my voice training I went back to Andrea James, who also teaches transgender women how to find their female voice. The voice is the hardest thing. You can look like Kate Moss but if you sound like James Earl Jones or Tony Curtis in *Some Like It Hot,* you got a problem. So I had to sound like a man who hasn't quite found his female voice. Understandably, Andrea had never had to do it the other way around, that is, make a woman sound like a man trying to sound like a woman. Andrea suggested I use 'the voice' as I went about my day.

"Well, suddenly I didn't want to talk anymore. I was so embarrassed and self-conscious trying to speak in my woman/man/woman voice, so instead

I found myself nodding or shaking my head or smiling in a "how ya doing" kind of way. *Anything* to keep from speaking."

More superficial yet equally important elements of Bree came from her hair, makeup, and wardrobe. Duncan Tucker describes the process:

"I had always been of the opinion that very meticulously thought-out and very feminine make-up, just a little bit too heavily applied, was the way to go," he says. "Our make-up artist, Lynn Campbell, was key make-up artist for *Sex and the City*, and Felicity worked closely with her. They contoured her face, accentuating the planes and angles, making her look more gaunt and bony. They used foundation that was just a shade off of what was appropriate for Felicity's coloring, to tell the story that Bree hadn't yet fully figured out how to use make-up.

"Jason Hayes, who did the wigs for *Hairspray* on Broadway, built us two amazing human hair wigs at a tenth of what they would normally cost, because of his belief in the project. We wouldn't have been able to afford them otherwise. He actually ended up taking a huge amount of hair out of the wigs, to thin them so they looked more like the hair of a man who decided to begin hormone therapy in mid-life.

"I asked costume designer Danny Glicker to think about catalogue-ordered clothes, since I imagined Bree was too self-conscious to go shopping in public, and to stick with pastels and ultra-feminine colors. He and Felicity soon discovered that Bree's favorite color was lavender, though she was also partial to mint, beige, and pink, that she wears scarves to conceal her neck, jackets to conceal her figure, long dresses to conceal her legs—all of Bree's clothing choices are about covering up."

Huffman observes, "Before sexual reassignment surgery, a candidate has to live as a woman for at least a year, before the person is cleared for the actual surgery. So I ask all the guys out there: think about waking up one morning and putting on a dress, make-up, and high heels and going to work or the grocery store or the bank. Can you imagine how terrifying that would be?

"I started to be able to comprehend the heroic journey gender dysphoric people take. *If* they are brave enough to fight for who they truly are, they are viewed as freaks and alienated from society. If they choose not to, they are alienated from themselves. I started the research for this movie thinking gender-dysphoric people were interesting but at best an odd anomaly. I ended the film knowing that these are some of the bravest people in the world."

"Felicity created a whole range of movements, tics, a walk, and a voice that made her an entirely different person," recalls producer Dungan. "I'll always remember when we were shooting in Phoenix and Bill Macy came to visit the set with their two young daughters. The youngest didn't recognize her mother in her full hair-makeup-costume-deep-voiced persona and started crying when Felicity tried to pick her up. I felt bad for Felicity as a mother, but I knew that we had really succeeded in her transformation at that point."

Huffman reports that the transformation ran so deep that vestiges of Bree stuck with her as *Desperate Housewives* went into production a couple of weeks after *Transamerica* wrapped.

"It was a culture shock," she says. "My voice was several octaves lower by the end of *Transamerica*. I honestly was having some confusion as to which one of the public restrooms I was supposed to use. Seriously, I would walk into the ladies' room and suddenly freeze—'Am I allowed in here?…yes!…no! This isn't my side…oh yes, it is, I *am* a girl'! Plus I kept answering to Marcia Cross's character, whose name is Bree. I'd hear an assistant director say, 'We are ready on set for Bree' and I would come flying out of my trailer."

"Actresses are under enormous pressure to look beautiful," concludes Dungan. "But they also want good, meaty parts, and Felicity's work in this film reminds me of what Charlize Theron went through for *Monster* and Hilary Swank's performance in *Boys Don't Cry,* as examples of actresses taking risks that have paid off. Felicity's total commitment to the reality of Bree is one of the things that I admire the most about her involvement in the film. The work she did on her voice and walk and mannerisms, getting coached by real transsexual women, was entirely her idea.

"It was also entirely Felicity's idea to wear the uncomfortable undergarments of a transsexual even when there was no way they could be seen."

Once shooting began, Huffman's greatest challenge was to maintain the character, though she reports the film's director helped with this.

"Duncan became my watchdog," she says. "Every time my voice went into a higher register, every time my gestures became too comfortably feminine, every time I lost Bree's walk, every nod of the head that wasn't totally Bree, Duncan would call me on it.

"I have to say, Duncan is a brave man, because if I wasn't snapping at him, denying the lapse, the producers were snapping at him, saying we couldn't afford another take just because my gesture was slightly off. But Duncan is tenacious. He wrote the script and loved Bree and when she didn't show up on the screen in all her authenticity he became a bulldog. I had to do it again. He pushed me and pushed me. It is a blessing to have a director who won't settle, and believes in your ability so much that he won't accept anything but the absolute, one hundred percent, truth from you. I settled into the character more as the film progressed, and consequently neither my husband nor my agent could recognize my voice when I called. My husband finally made a rule that I couldn't talk to him 'in character.' It was too weird."

ON TRANSSEXUALITY
AND TRANSAMERICA
BY DUNCAN TUCKER

The plumbing works, and so does the electricity.
—*Kate Bornstein, transsexual actress, educator,*
and activist, when asked by a TV talk-show
host if she could reach orgasm with "that vagina"

When I began working on the outline of *Transamerica* I didn't know much about people of transsexual experience. I read several memoirs, including *Conundrum,* by Jan Morris, who, as James Morris, fathered five children and documented the first expedition to climb Everest; *Second Serve,* by tennis champion Renée Richards; *The Christine Jorgensen Story,* whose eponymous author was a transsexual pioneer; *My Story,* by the gorgeous trans nude Playboy model and Bond girl Caroline Cossey.

The trans community is necessarily self-protective. It took a lot of work to meet and gain the trust of a number of transwomen in New York City, where I live. They were brave and generous to share their stories with me. I met transsexual lesbian lovers (straight friends before transition); a selfless trans woman surgeon still married to her wonderful, supportive wife; a transwoman who lived with and cared for her aging mother, but whose siblings and children wouldn't talk to her; a stunning, silky-voiced trans blonde who spent her days lounging by the pool in an exclusive suburban country club, hunting for a rich husband. The stories they told me were hilarious, tragic, surprising, brave—full of unexpected reversals and startling moments of grace. They gave me a huge reservoir of raw material for stories and characters. I could write and direct nothing but transsexual movies the rest of my life and barely ripple those waters.

Stealth Transsexual: A Transsexual Secret Agent

I was surprised by how often, when I met a transwoman at a café or restaurant, I was unable to recognize her as anything but a G.G. (a genetic girl). When a transwoman could be read, it was as likely to be a choice she'd made as it was a handicap she couldn't fix. We tend only to spot the transpeople among us who do not pass, or who are only partway through their transitions. I wrote Bree Osborne as a stealth transsexual, and I knew from the outset that she wouldn't be played by a man in a dress. I wanted to tell the truth about Bree, and that meant honoring her identity as a woman, honoring her destination—instead of leaving her stuck in what she was leaving behind.

I knew I'd have to find a special kind of actress, a transformative actress. When Felicity Huffman accepted the role I was overjoyed. She's an artist of great imagination, courage, and empathy. Starting with the clay of my words, she brought a complex and contradictory, funny and frustrating, startlingly alive and kicking trans woman to vivid life. As well as I've come to know Felicity, I still find myself missing Bree. That's great acting.

> Jesus made me this way for a reason, so I could
> suffer and be reborn, the way he was.
> —*Sabrina Claire Osborne*

You've got to be sneaky to be subversive. *Transamerica's* main character is a transsexual, yet the film is not about transsexuality. At heart it's an old-fashioned movie about family, self-acceptance, and the longing to be loved. The plot is structured along the lines of classic road movies, with some recognizable road movie paradigms, yet the two protagonists whose lives it celebrates are anything but familiar. Their lives haven't been easy. They're different, misunderstood, and alone. It's strange how we all want the same things—family, love, home—and yet there's no such thing as "normal." Bree and Toby have had hard lives, but they're survivors. In *Transamerica* I tried to tell a story that, like life, was sometimes funny and sometimes heartbreaking. I hoped viewers would leave the theater feeling a little bit more in love with life's richness and possibility. And I hoped to transport a wide range of people into the minds and hearts of two human beings they might ordinarily look upon as untouchables, or more likely, not look upon at all.

Two Kinds of People:
1) People who think there are two kinds of people.
2) The other kind.

We construct a universe of dualisms. Black/white, blue state/red state, gay/straight, good/evil, male/female. Seeing the world this way may be rooted in our bilaterally symmetrical anatomy. Perhaps if we were built like starfish, we'd divide the world into kinds of five.

At any rate, life isn't really made up of either/ors, and all too often we mistake our two-color maps for the far subtler territories they represent. Gender, I've learned, is not the same as anatomy. Like so much else in the universe, it is a continuum. The signs and signifiers of gender are more fluid than fixed, and always open to interpretation. Is a woman who plays baseball, shuns make-up, and is an ace parallel parker the same gender as Marilyn Monroe? Is Prince the same gender as Sylvester Stallone?

Think of gender as a rowboat: some people perch carefully in the center, others sit to one side or the other, still others lean out precariously over the edge. And some people cannot keep from tipping the boat over completely.

★ ★ ★

A Brief Transsexual Lexicon

High-Intensity Transsexual: Twenty people out of every million. Someone motivated to undergo the cosmetic and medical procedures necessary to change sex.

Transgendered: Anyone who doesn't sit in the center of the boat.

Gender Dysphoria (a k a Gender Identity Disorder, or GID): A state in which one's anatomy does not correspond to one's gender.

SRS: Sexual Reassignment Surgery. The cure for gender dysphoria.

MTF (Male to Female) **Transsexual:** A Woman made by God with a little help from Man. An MTF transsexual is sometimes called a trans woman.

FTM (Female to Male) **Transsexual:** A Man made by God with a little help from Woman. An FTM transsexual is sometimes called a trans man.

Transpeople (trans women, trans men): Human beings who happen to be trans.

Trannie: A word best used only if you are one.

Transvestite: Clothes make the woman.

Intersexual: A person with partially or fully developed male and female sexual organs. The term "intersexual" is preferred to "hermaphrodite."

Transsensual: Sexual attraction to transpeople.

Passing: What happens when others take you for what you truly are.

Being read: What happens when they do not.

G.G. ("genetic girl" or "genuine girl"): A term used by women of trans experience in referring to women of the other sort.

Genetically Gifted: For an MTF, being of small stature, with small hands and feet, delicate features, and a slender frame. For an FTM, the opposite.

Proper pronouns: Respect and metaphysics dictate the use of pronouns that correspond to the gender with which the referenced person self-identifies. A male to female transsexual woman is always "she," never "he," and vice versa.

Tucking: A temporary measure.

How to tuck: Stand with your legs apart. Push the penis and testicles down and back, then bring the legs firmly together. Hitch up your pantyhose and reinforced girdle to bind and moor all loose objects to the pelvic hull.

Monthly nosebleeds: Vicarious menstruation.

Baldness: A genetic drawback that can sometimes be corrected with estrogen therapy.

Baldness: A genetic gift that can sometimes be acquired with testosterone therapy.

Sexuality: Who you desire and, according to some, what you do about it. Sexuality is unrelated to gender identity.

Sex: Something easier to change than your sexuality.

Normal: A concept largely irrelevant to anyone's life.

CAST AND FILMMAKER CREDITS

THE WEINSTEIN COMPANY and IFC FILMS Present

TRANSAMERICA

CAST

Laura Kinney	Allie Mickelson	Taylor	Stella Maeve
Bree	Felicity Huffman	Little Girl	Teala Dunn
Toby	Kevin Zegers	Taylor's Father	Jim Frangione
Elizabeth	Fionnula Flanagan	Kelly	Kelly O'Connell
Margaret	Elizabeth Peña	Calpernia	Calpernia Addams
Calvin	Graham Greene	Sandi	Sandi Alexander
Murray	Burt Young	Melissa	Melissa Sklarz
Sydney	Carrie Preston	Felicia	Felicia Kittles
Arletty	Venita Evans	David	David Harrison
Alex	Jon Budinoff	Sammy	Forrie Smith
Bobby Jensen	Raynor Scheine	Phoenix Lady	Elayne Stein
Hitchhiker	Grant Monohon	Phoenix Cop	Amy Povich
Mary Ellen	Bianca Leigh	Male Nurse	Burton Elias
Dr. Spikowsky	Danny Burstein	Filipino Nurse	Cecy
Police Sergeant	Craig Bockhorn	Wayne	Matt Young
Voice Coach	Andrea James	Ms. Swallow	Barbara Hubbard Barron
Fernando	Maurice Orozco	Gas Station Dog	Lou Lou
NYC Cop	Paul Borghese	Lucky	Zero T. Poodle
Tennessee Waitress	Kate Bayley		

FILMMAKERS

Written and directed by	Duncan Tucker	Music Composed and Performed by	David Mansfield
Produced by	Linda Moran	Costume Design	Danny Glicker
	Rene Bastian	Music Supervisor	Doug Bernheim
	Sebastian Dungan	Casting	Eve Battaglia
Executive Producer	William H. Macy	Production Manager	Elinyisia Mosha
Associate Producer	Lucy Cooper	Key Hair & Make-Up	Lynn Campbell
Director of Photography	Stephen Kazmierski	Location Manager	Michele Baker
Sound Recordist	Griffin Richardson	Supervising Sound Editor	Lou Bertini
Editor	Pam Wise, A.C.E.		
Production Design	Mark White		

ABOUT THE WRITER/DIRECTOR

Duncan Tucker has worked in a variety of jobs in a variety of fields. His first love is storytelling, with music and pictures running neck and neck as close seconds. One day he realized that by making movies he could arrange a polygamous marriage of all three.

Duncan's short film *The Mountain King* (2001) played in more than thirty film festivals worldwide and received a nationwide theatrical release in a program of four short films titled *Boys to Men*, distributed by Jour de Fete/Rialto Films. *Transamerica* was his feature debut.

AWARDS

Best Film, Berlin Film Festival (Siegesalle Jury Award), Woodstock Film Festival (Audience Award), San Francisco Frameline Film Festival (Audience Award), Glitter Awards (Foreign Gay and Lesbian Film Festival Award), GLAAD (Gay and Lesbian Alliance Against Defamation) Media Awards (limited release)

Best Indie Film, Fort Lauderdale Film Festival

Special Citation for *Achievement in Independent Film,* Phoenix Film Festival

Best Feature, Goldeneye (Jamaica) Film Festival

Best First Screenplay, Independent Spirit Award

Best Screenplay, Deauville Film Festival

Felicity Huffman received *Best Actress* awards from the Golden Globes, Independent Spirit Awards, National Board of Review, Glitter Awards, Tribeca Film Festival, San Diego Film Festival, Aspen Film Festival, Mill Valley Film Festival, and Florida International Film Festival, and she will be honored by the Palm Springs International Film Festival. She was also honored by Movieline's *Hollywood Life* with its *Breakthrough Performance* award.